Jump-Start Method for Guitar
Volume 1

ISBN: 978-0-578-01042-7

Contents

Introduction

As a teacher for the last 13 years, one of the things that I've seen students struggle with the most is music theory. I have read a lot of books on music theory, and I have found most all of them very informative. The only problem is that they often take for granted that the reader is already an intermediate to advanced musician. For beginning guitarists, many of these books can be very hard to follow.

Most students who are starting out on guitar want to be able to make chords, play songs, jam with others in a band, but they're not interested in delving deeply into the theory behind the chords yet. Students often ask me "what theory do I need to know just to get by?" If you're like those students, this book is for you. It will help you get started building and strumming chords with just the little bit of theory that you need to get by. But don't be fooled - it's a useful and powerful "little bit".

I've met many musicians, who, if you asked them to play an E-minor-7-flat-5 ($Em^{7(b5)}$) chord, would look at you with a blank expression. And who can blame them - it sounds complicated! But you'll be surprised to know that by learning "just enough" theory, you can whip out an $Em^{7(b5)}$ chord whenever you need one.

Some people try to memorize chord shapes. Since there are hundreds of possible chords that you can make on the guitar, this is a little like trying to memorize every single answer to the addition problems in a math book, but not learning how to add. It works great as long as the problem you're solving is one you've memorized the answer to. But if you know how to add, then you can solve any addition problem you encounter. And it's the same with playing chords on the guitar. Instead of memorizing the shapes, you'll memorize a few simple rules that will let you create virtually any chord. These are the kinds of skills that this book will be focusing on.

In this book you will learn how to build hundreds of chords through a simple "5-1-3" system which I have laid out for you with many illustrations and step-by-step instructions. You will also learn how the notes are distributed throughout the guitar and how they relate to building chords. This will give you a huge advantage in learning more advanced concepts, build confidence in your playing ability, and jump-start you on your way to playing the guitar.

Before we get started making chords, you will have to know how to read this chord chart

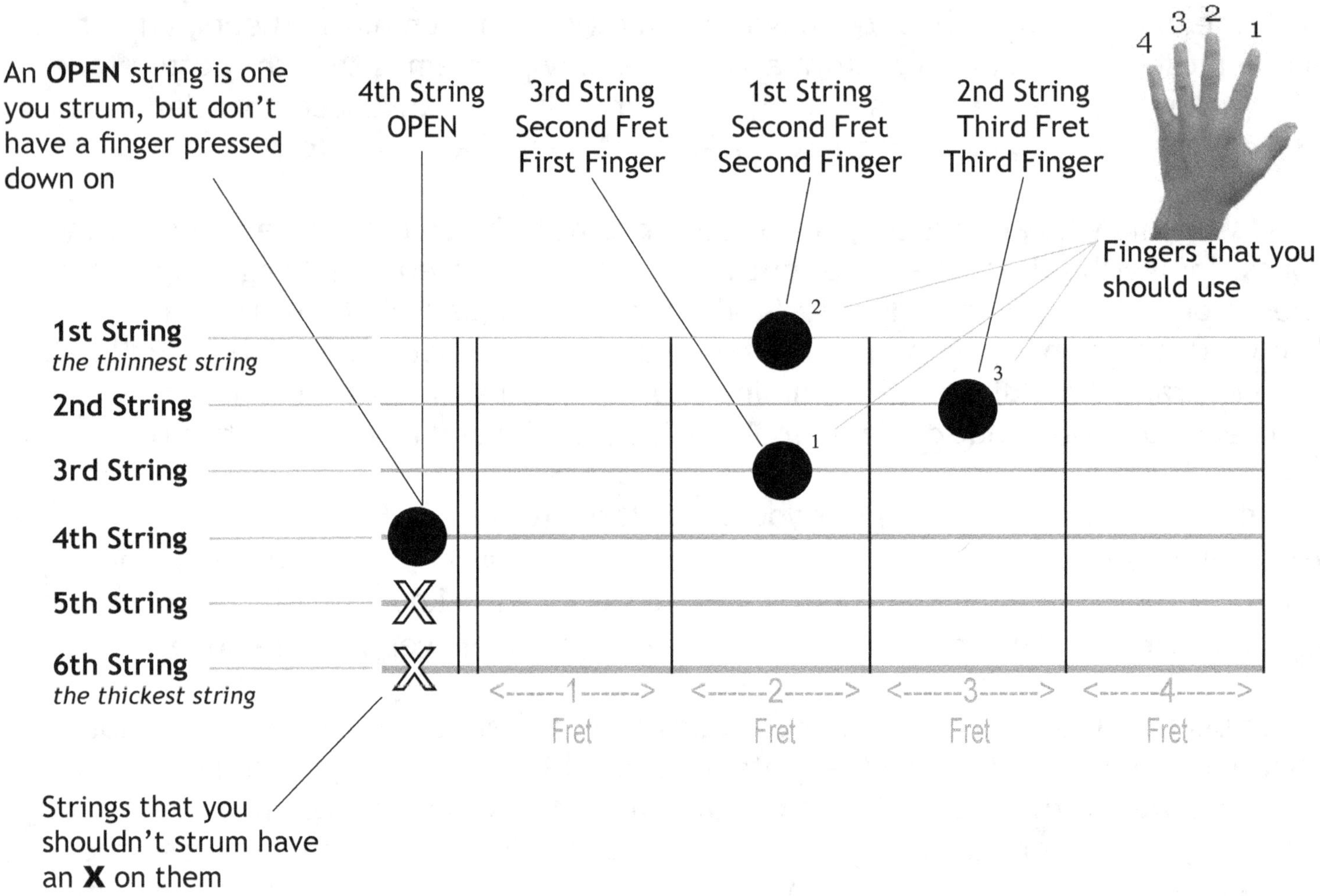

An **OPEN** string is one you strum, but don't have a finger pressed down on

4th String OPEN

3rd String Second Fret First Finger

1st String Second Fret Second Finger

2nd String Third Fret Third Finger

Fingers that you should use

1st String
the thinnest string

2nd String

3rd String

4th String

5th String

6th String
the thickest string

<-----1----->
Fret

<-----2----->
Fret

<-----3----->
Fret

<-----4----->
Fret

Strings that you shouldn't strum have an **X** on them

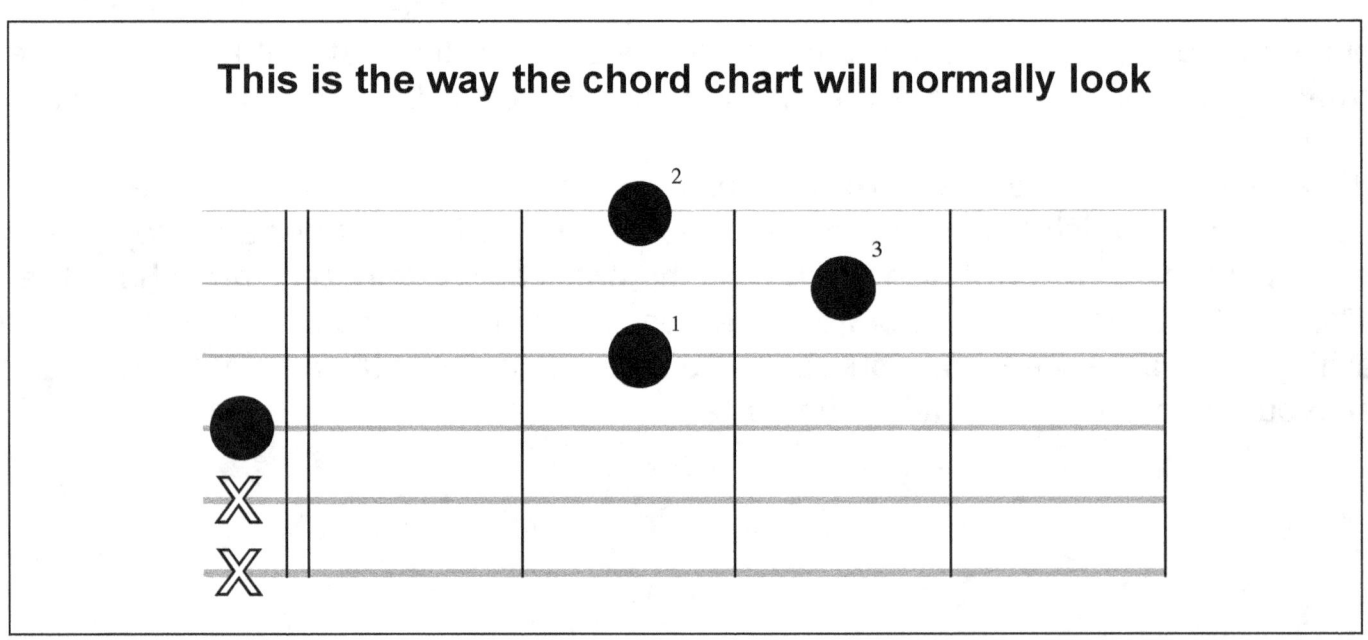

This is the way the chord chart will normally look

Major Chords
The Three "Home Chords"

Example 1.1

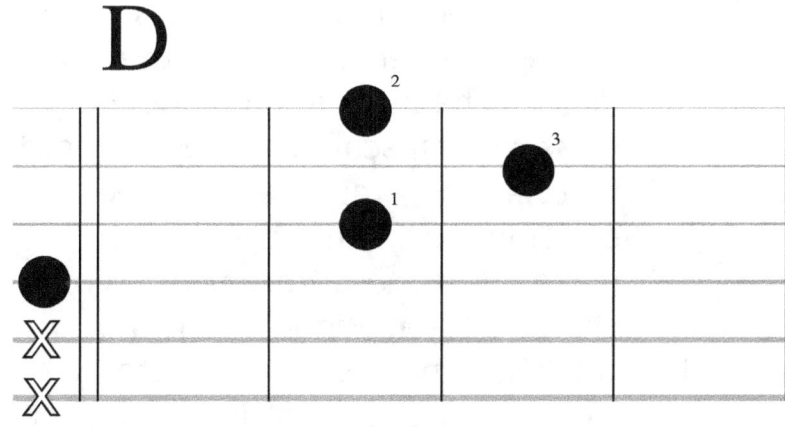

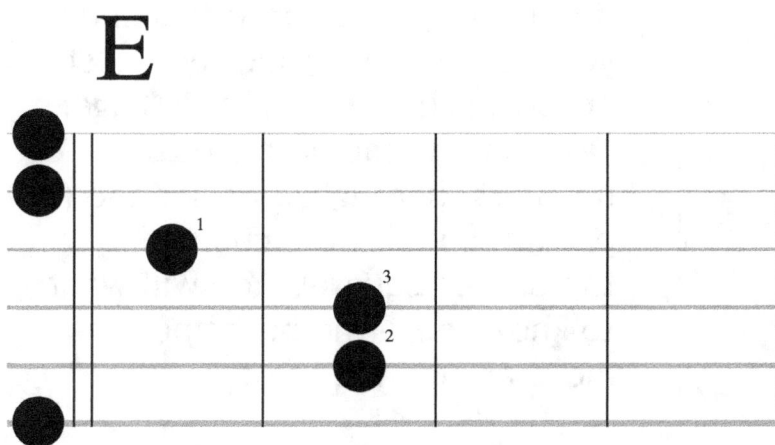

The first thing we'll be doing is learning these three Major chords, which I'll refer to as the "home chords": **D, A, and E.** The small numbers will tell you what fingers to use. Make sure to practice the fingerings as indicated on the charts.

Pay attention to which strings you strum (the open strings and the ones you're pressing your fingers on) and which strings you don't (the strings marked with an "X").

Don't expect all of the notes to ring out perfectly at first. It can take a little while to develop the callouses, strength and flexibility to play these chords well. If you're just starting out on the guitar you can expect that all of the chords in this book will feel uncomfortable and awkward at first.

Scale Degrees
The Three "Home Chords" with Scale Degrees

Example 1.2

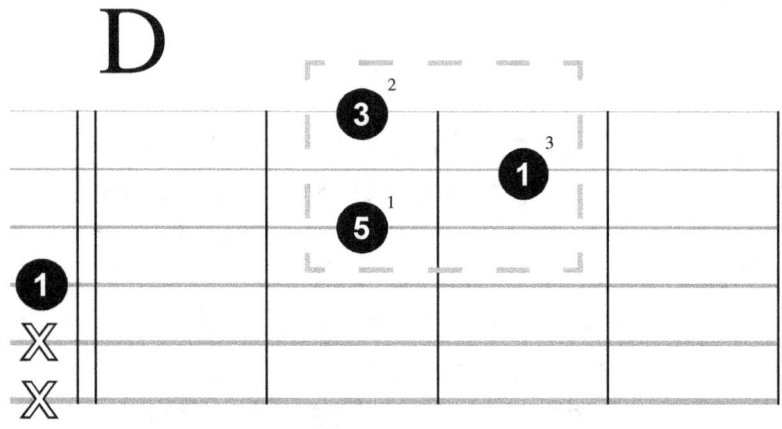

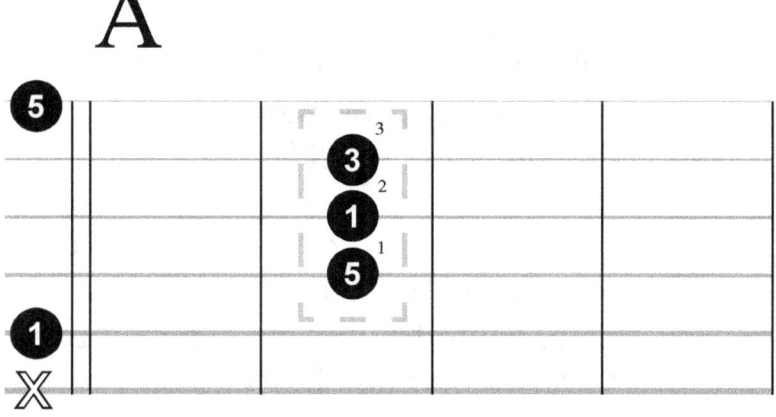

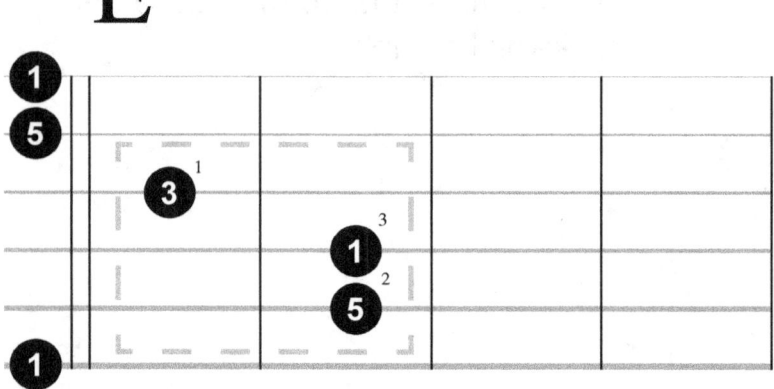

In Example 1.2, the first thing that you're probably wondering is, what do the numbers inside the circles mean? The numbers represent what we call scale degrees or chord factors. These numbers are the building blocks that are used to make all of the different types of chords (Major, Minor, etc.). Now why these numbers are located where they are is not important for the time being. For now, all that you need to know is where they are and that we can use them to build chords.

First we will start by making the three Home Chords in Example 1.2 and locating where the ones, threes and fives are in each of the three chords. For example, if you start with the D chord and use the fingerings indicated (by the small black numbers on the chart), the 5 (or 5th) is under your first finger. The 3 (or 3rd) is under your second finger and the 1 (1st or root) is under your third finger. Take time to memorize these numbers thoroughly. Notice the ($\begin{smallmatrix}3\\1\\5\end{smallmatrix}$) pattern on all three chords inside the dashed squares. You will want to know these the best since they move around the most.

Flats & Sharps

Example 1.3

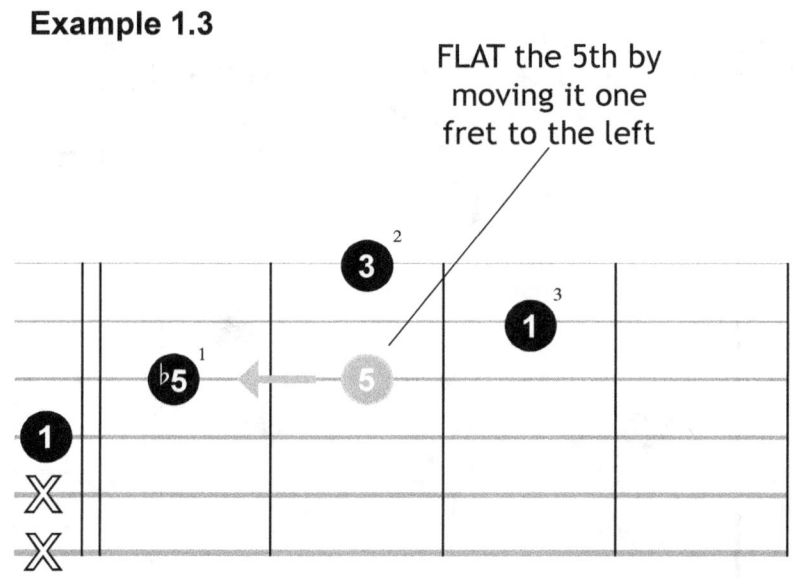

FLAT the 5th by moving it one fret to the left

Once you feel like you know the three home chords and where their scale degrees are fairly well, you can start learning how to **flat** (♭) and **sharp** (♯) the scale degrees. To **flat** a scale degree, we move it one fret to the **left**. To **sharp** a scale degree, we move it one fret to the **right**.

In Example 1.3, we **flat** the 5th by moving it one fret to the left. Remember to keep your other fingers pressed down on the 1st and the 3rd while doing this.

Example 1.4

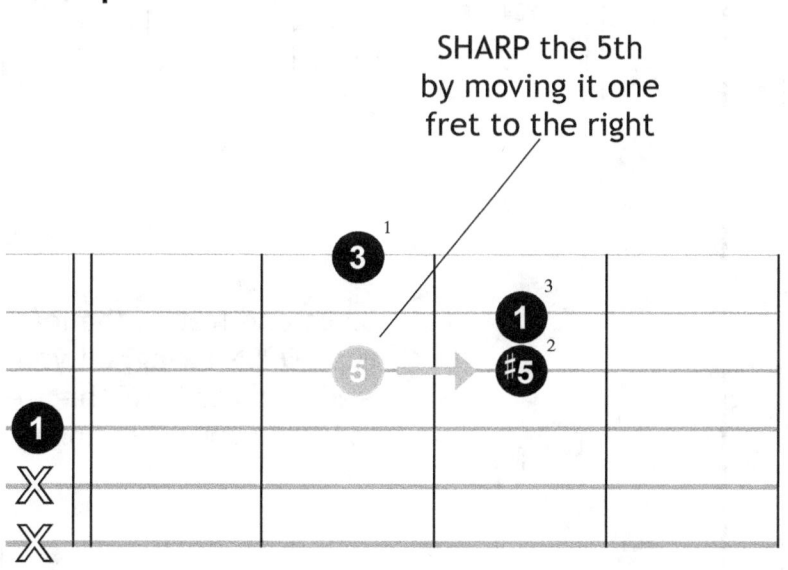

SHARP the 5th by moving it one fret to the right

Now let's try Example 1.4, and **sharp** the 5th by moving it one fret to the right. Notice that you have to change fingerings for this to be possible. If you've forgotten the D chord fingerings, go back and review the previous examples.

Home Chords

Example 1.5

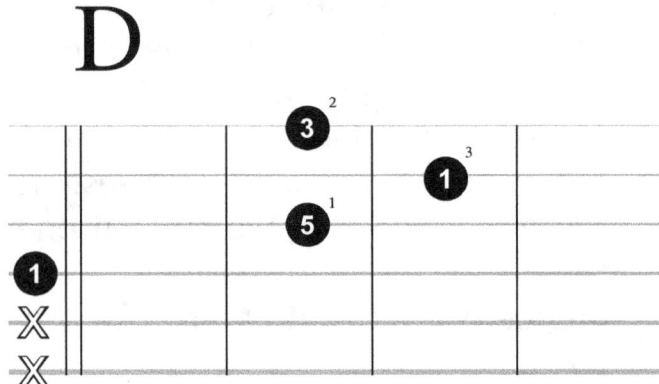

D

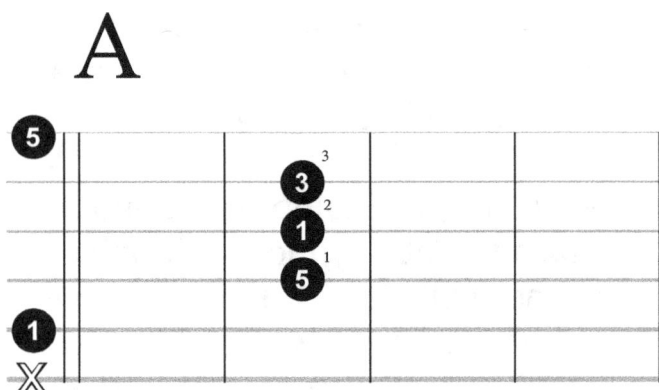

A

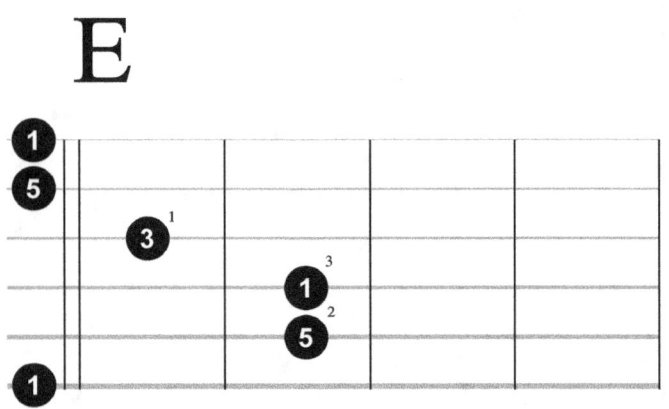

E

Minor Chords

Example 1.6

FLAT the 3rd by moving it one fret to the left

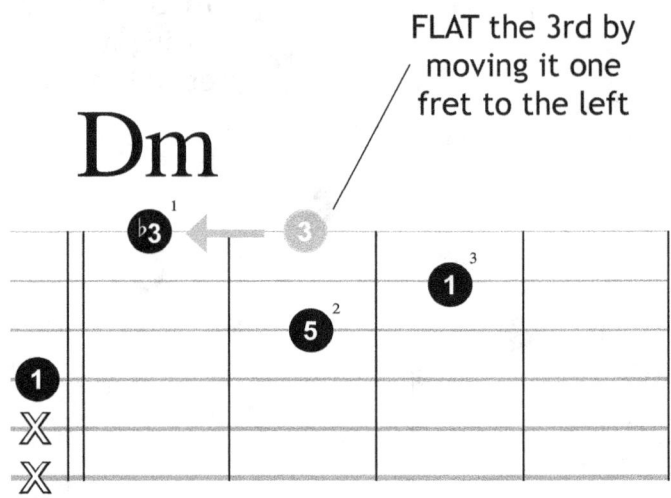

Dm

FLAT the 3rd by moving it one fret to the left

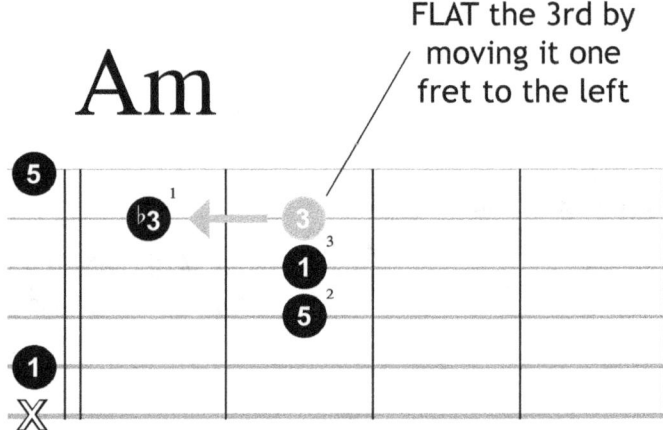

Am

Since one fret to the left is an OPEN string, all you need to do to FLAT the 3rd is lift up your first finger

Em

Minor Chords
1 - ♭3 - 5

The 2nd chords that we will be learning (in Examples 1.5 and 1.6) are called the Minor chords. You can create these chords by making the three Home Chords, D, A, and E, and then flatting the 3rd, making the chord formula: 1 - ♭3 - 5. This is the formula for all Minor chords.

Practice going back and forth between D and Dm a few times. Pay attention to the fingering numbers - notice that sometimes you have to change your fingering in order to make the new chord. Now do the same with the other chords. Sometimes you will have to shift your fingering and other times you won't.

Now (for fun) try going through the following examples of the 12 Bar Blues. Count to four and strum on each count. If you're having trouble switching chords fast enough, try to keep counting to four while you play, but only strum on the one. This will give you a little more time to think. It also helps to use a metronome to pace yourself.

12 Bar A-Major Blues

A

:1	2	3	4	1	2	3	4	1	2	3	4	1	2	3	4

strum   *strum*   *strum*

D   A

1	2	3	4	1	2	3	4	1	2	3	4	1	2	3	4

E   D   A   E

1	2	3	4	1	2	3	4	1	2	3	4	1	2	3	4:

12 Bar A-Minor Blues

Am

:1	2	3	4	1	2	3	4	1	2	3	4	1	2	3	4

strum   *strum*   *strum*

Dm   Am

1	2	3	4	1	2	3	4	1	2	3	4	1	2	3	4

Em   Dm   Am   Em

1	2	3	4	1	2	3	4	1	2	3	4	1	2	3	4:

Home Chords

Diminished Chords

Example 1.7

Example 1.8

D

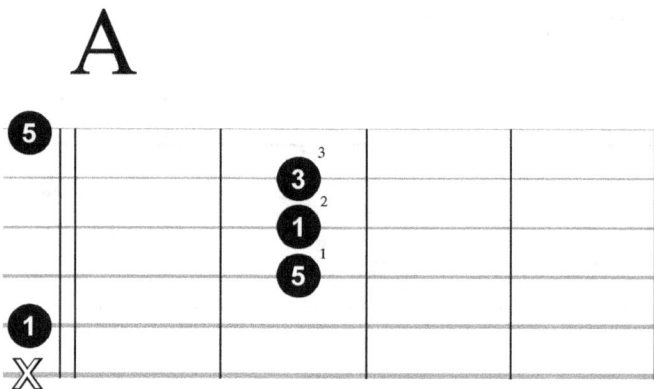

A

E

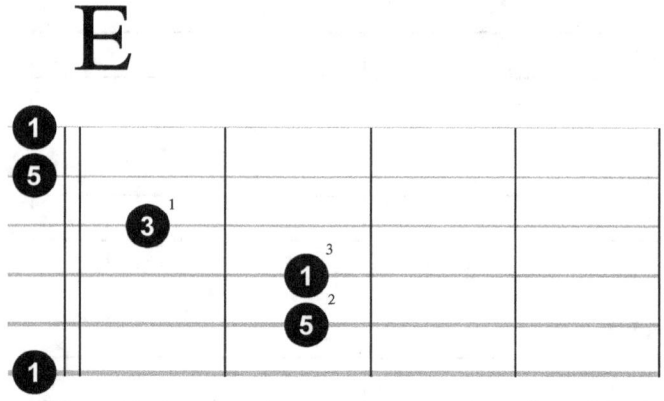

Ddim

FLAT the 3rd and the 5th by moving them one fret to the left

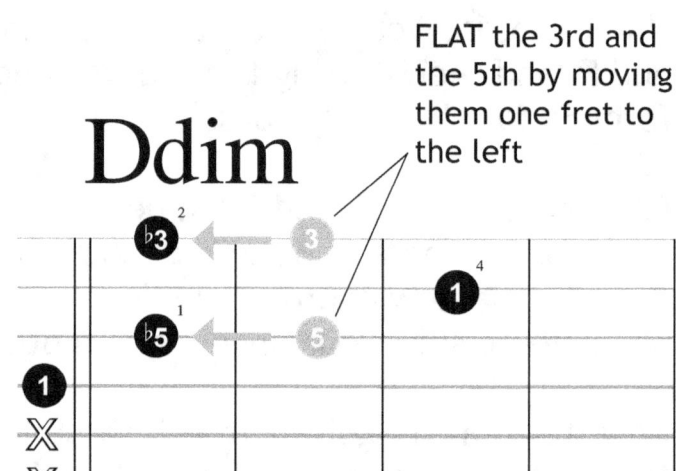

Adim

FLAT the 3rd and the 5th by moving them one fret to the left

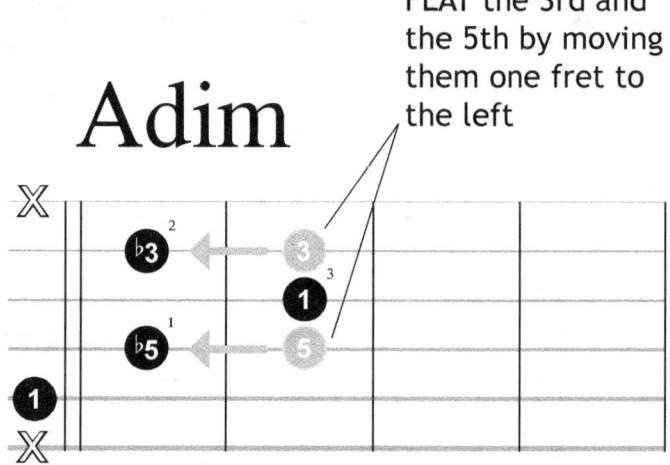

Edim

FLAT the 3rd and the 5th by moving them one fret to the left

Remember: with this chord, all you need to do to FLAT the 3rd is lift up your finger

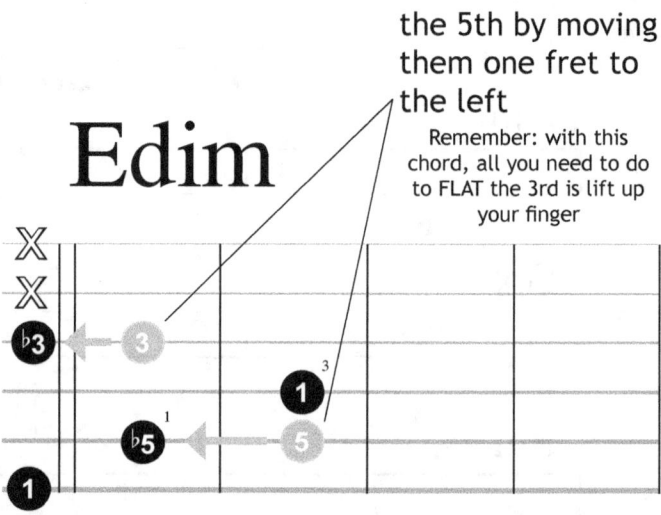

Diminished Chords
1 - ♭3 - ♭5

The next chords, in Examples 1.7 and 1.8, are called the Diminished chords. These may sound a little unusual to you, but they can be very musical in the proper context. These chords require a lot of stretching and many people find them difficult to make at first. Keep practicing - it will get easier.

To make the Diminished chord, start with the Home Chords, D, A, and E, and then flat the 3rd and the 5th, making the chord formula: 1 - ♭3 - ♭5. This is the formula for all Diminished chords. Again, pay attention to the fingering numbers - sometimes you have to change your fingering in order to make the new chord.

You can practice the progression examples below to get used to the sound of the Diminished chords in a musical context.

Diminished Chord Strumming

A		Adim	A				D		Ddim	D			
:1	2	3	4	1	2	3	4	1	2	3	4	1	2	3	4

strum   *strum*   *strum*

E		Edim	E				A		Adim	A			
1	2	3	4	1	2	3	4	1	2	3	4	1	2	3	4:

Home Chords

Augmented Chords

Example 1.9

Example 1.10

D

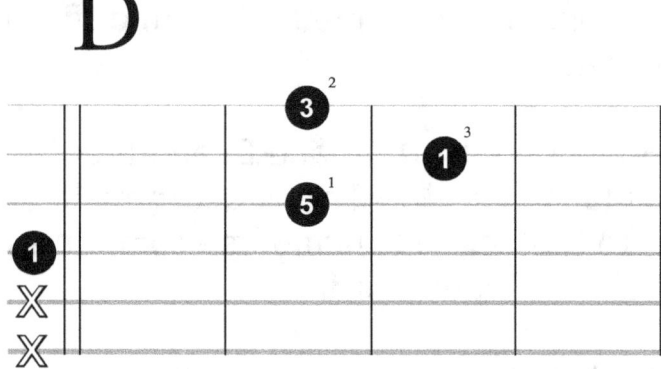

Daug

SHARP the 5th by moving it one fret to the right

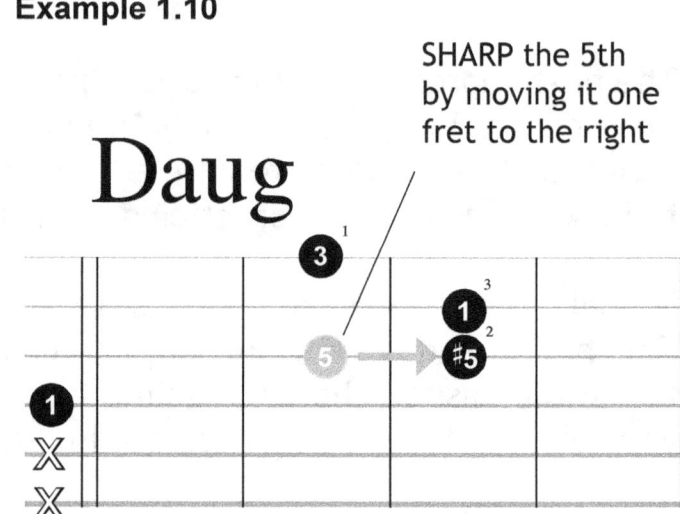

A

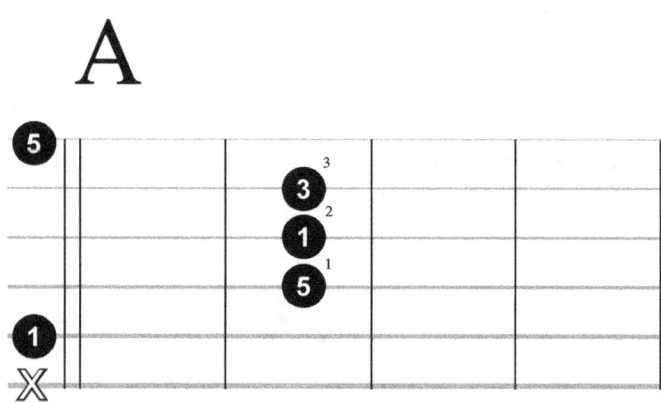

Aaug

SHARP the 5th by moving it one fret to the right

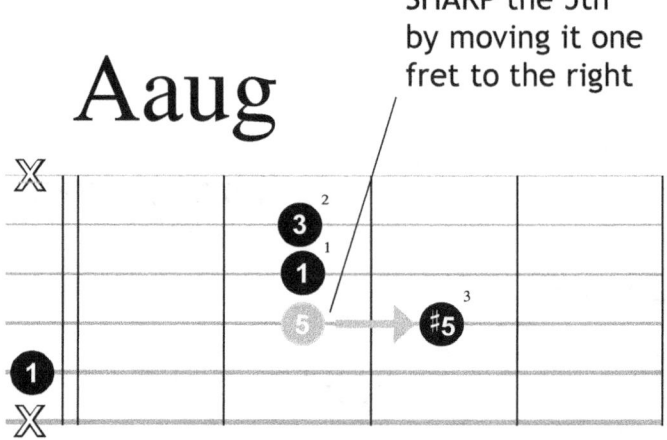

E

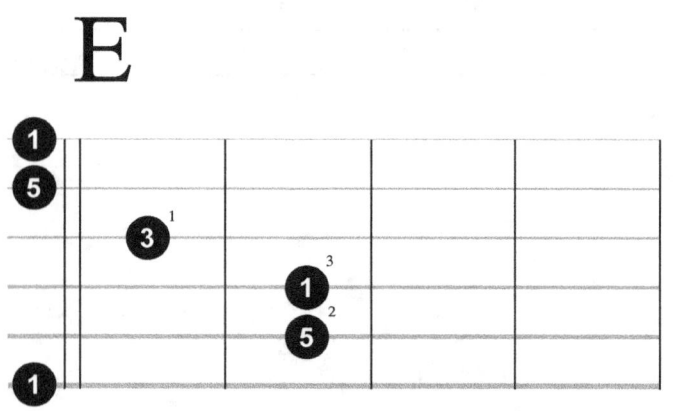

Eaug

SHARP the 5th by moving it one fret to the right

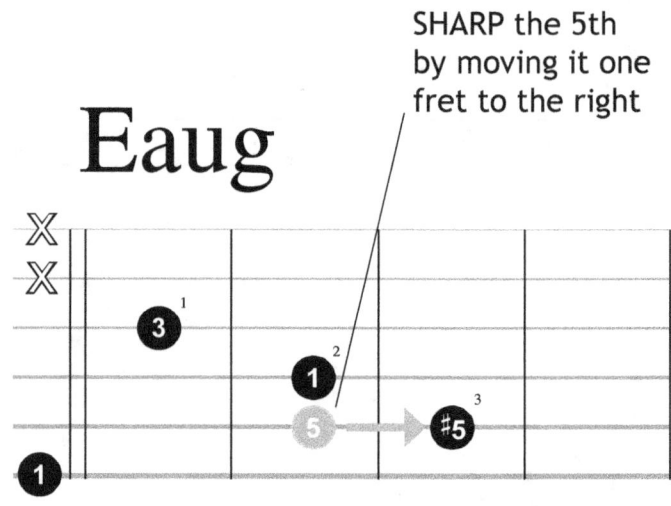

Augmented Chords
1 - 3 - #5

Now let's try making the Augmented chords, as seen in Examples 1.9 and 1.10, by making the Home D, A and E chords and sharping the 5th.   This gives us the chord formula: 1 - 3 - #5. This is the formula for all Augmented chords.

Practice switching back and forth between the Home chords and the Augmented chords to see how the 5th moves around. As always, pay attention to the fingering numbers - sometimes you have to change your fingering to make the new chord.

Next, try playing the following example:

Augmented Chord Strumming

D				Daug				D				Daug			
:1	2	3	4	1	2	3	4	1	2	3	4	1	2	3	4

strum   *strum*   *strum*

A				Aaug				A				Aaug			
1	2	3	4	1	2	3	4	1	2	3	4	1	2	3	4:

E				Eaug				E				Eaug			
1	2	3	4	1	2	3	4	1	2	3	4	1	2	3	4:

Review
4 Formulas = 12 Chords

Example 1.11

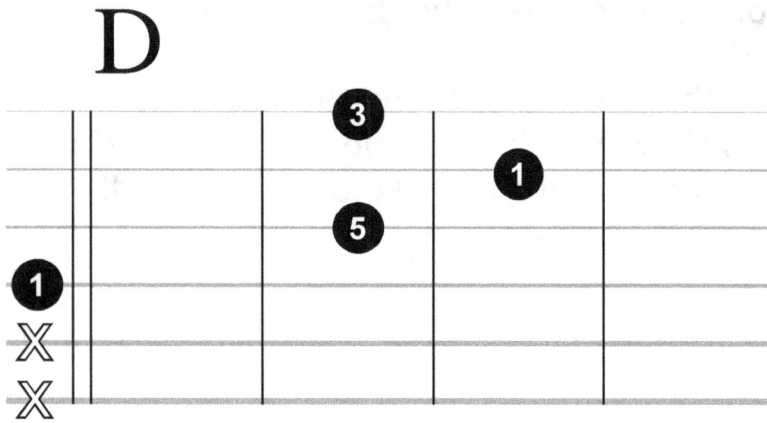

D

A

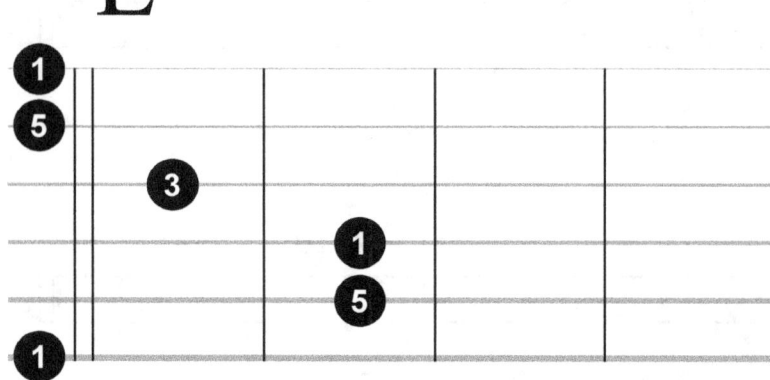

E

Now we've come full-circle back to the Major ("Home") chords. Notice that in Example 1.11, the fingerings are not shown this time. That's because now it's time for you to try to build the chords on your own.

If you can't remember one of the fingerings that you learned, try to make up your own fingerings that you feel comfortable with.

Remember that:
flat (♭) = 1 fret left
sharp (♯) = 1 fret right

With that information and your knowledge of the Home chords, the list of chord formulas below should be all that you need to build the twelve different chords that we've covered:

1	3	5	Major
1	♭3	5	Minor
1	♭3	♭5	Diminished
1	3	♯5	Augmented

SECTION 2
Sliding 3-Note Chords

Example 2 shows the names of the notes on the second, third and fourth strings of the guitar. In this section, we're going to learn how to slide our chord formulas up and down the neck of the guitar to create new chords. The notes on these strings will determine the letter name of our chord when we slide it.

The letter name of the chord	Type of chord
$\mathbf{D}$	$\mathbf{m}^{7(\flat 5)}$

You may notice that the musical alphabet is just like the regular alphabet from A to G, with some sharps or flats in between. On each string the alphabet starts with the open note on the string, continues up each fret until it reaches G#, then starts over at A. Every note has a sharp, except B and E and each note has a flat except C and F, so:

The musical alphabet for sharps is: A - A# - B - C - C# - D - D# - E - F - F# - G - G#
And the musical alphabet for flats is: A - B♭ - B - C - D♭ - D - E♭ - E - F - G♭ - G - A♭

Example 2

	1		3		5		7		9			12		
2nd String B	C	C#/D♭	D	D#/E♭	E	F	F#/G♭	G	G#/A♭	A	A#/B♭	B	C	C#/D♭
3rd String G	G#/A♭	A	A#/B♭	B	C	C#/D♭	D	D#/E♭	E	F	F#/G♭	G	G#/A♭	A
4th String D	D#/E♭	E	F	F#/G♭	G	G#/A♭	A	A#/B♭	B	C	C#/D♭	D	D#/E♭	E

So far, there has been no need to worry about note names, since all of the chords have been D, A or E chords of one type or another. But now, if we know the notes on these three strings, we will be able to take all of the chords that we have learned so far and make chords of any letter name that we want by sliding them up and down the neck - **giving us hundreds of possible chords!**

For example, if we slide the D chord five frets to the right, it turns into a G chord (see Example 2.1A on the next page). And the beautiful thing is, **it still feels and looks like a D chord** and the scale degrees will all slide up with the chord also. Then if I want to convert my new G chord into a G minor chord, I can just pretend that it's a D chord and flat the third.

Spend some time memorizing the notes on the strings and then study Examples 2.1A through 2.3C.

Examples 2.1A, B & C show how to slide the three-note D chord formulas up and down the neck of the guitar. Notice that I have put the note names only on the string that has the 1st (root) scale degree on it. That's all we need to figure out the letter name of our new chords. The chord formulas we learned in the previous sections determine the TYPE of chord we're making and the location of the root (1) gives us the NAME of the chord. Note that in the examples below, all of the open strings are X-ed out. We can't slide notes that are on an open string, so you won't strum these strings when sliding the chord.

Examples 2.1A, B & C

Whatever note the 1 is on will be the letter name of the chord

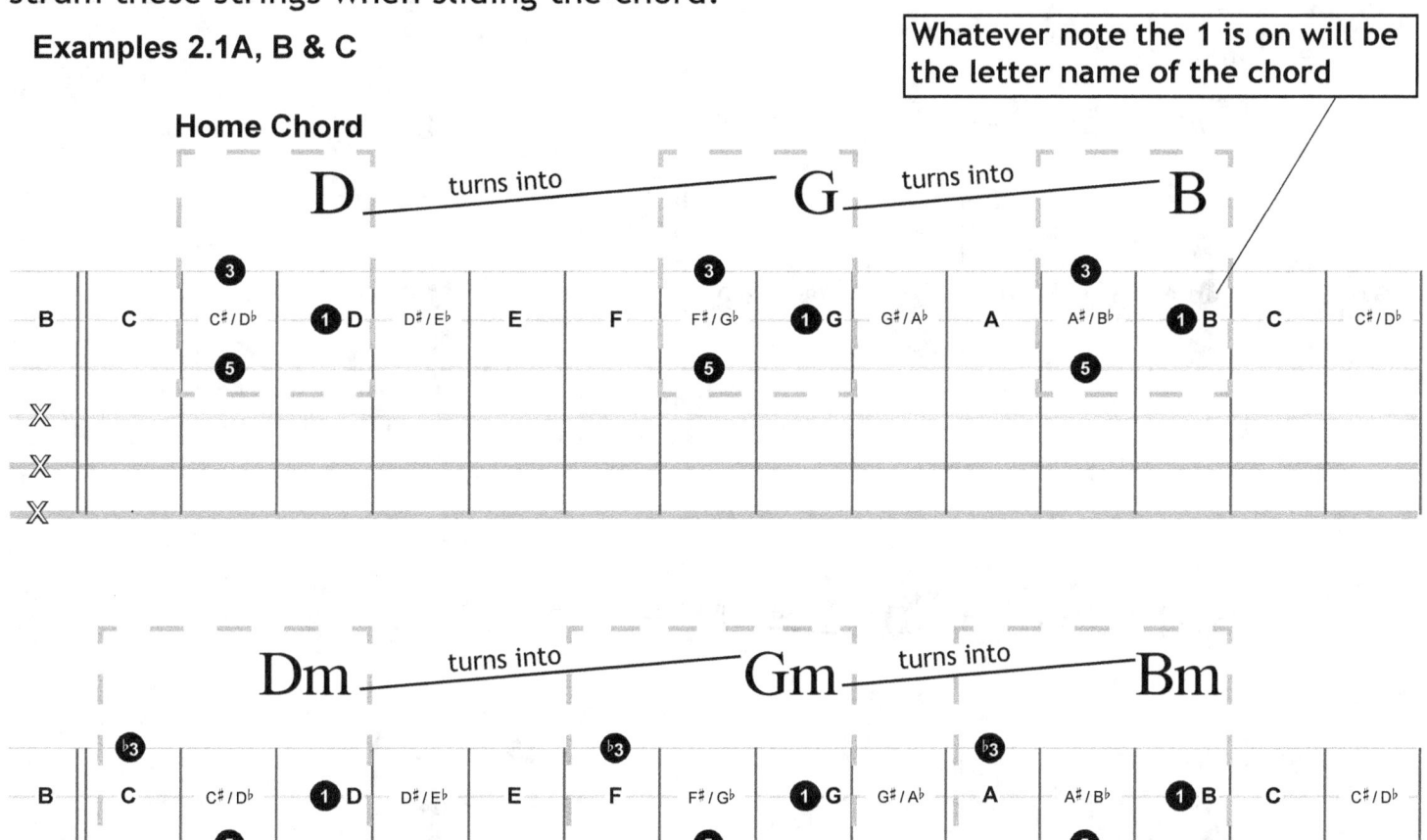

Now let's try the sliding the A chord to create some new chords. Notice that I still have all the open strings X-ed out - you shouldn't strum those. This time we only need the notes on the **third** string (where the root (1) of the A Chord is located) to find the letter name of the new chords.

Examples 2.2A, B & C

Whatever note the 1 is on will be the letter name of the chord

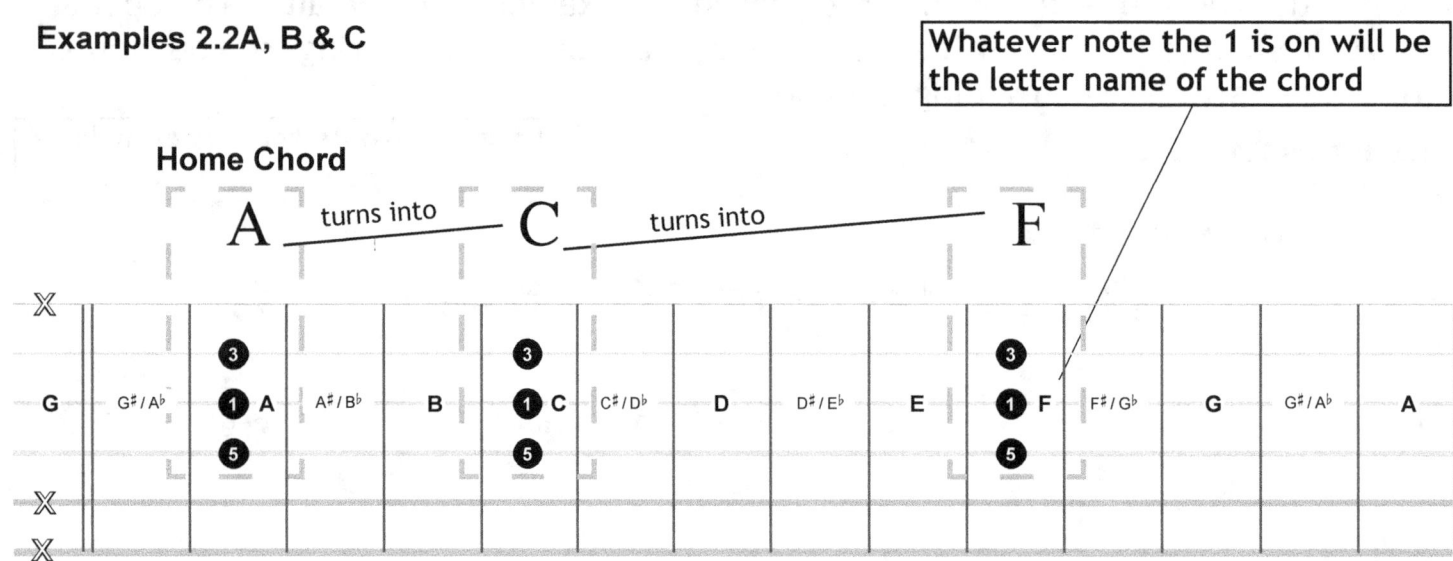

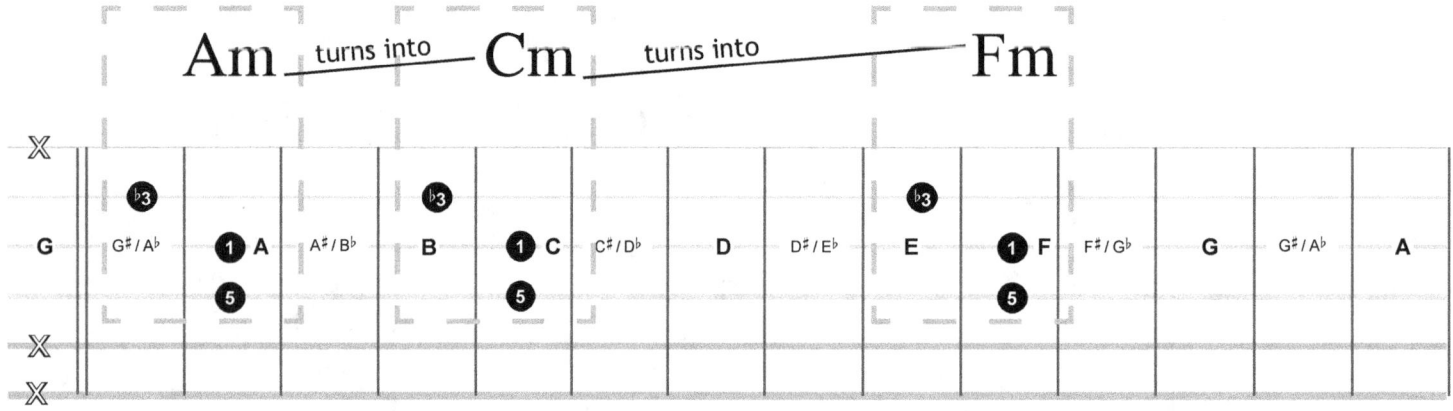

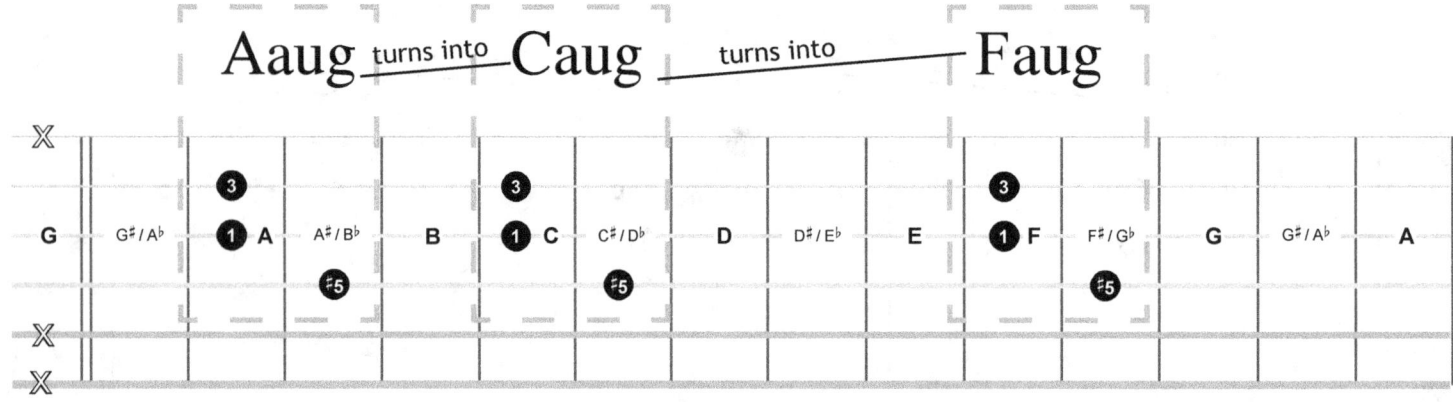

Next, of course, we're going to make some new chords by sliding the E chords around. The open strings that you shouldn't strum are X-ed out and now we need the notes on the **fourth** string (where the root (1) of the E Chord is located) to find the letter name of the new chords.

Examples 2.3A, B & C

Whatever note the 1 is on will be the letter name of the chord

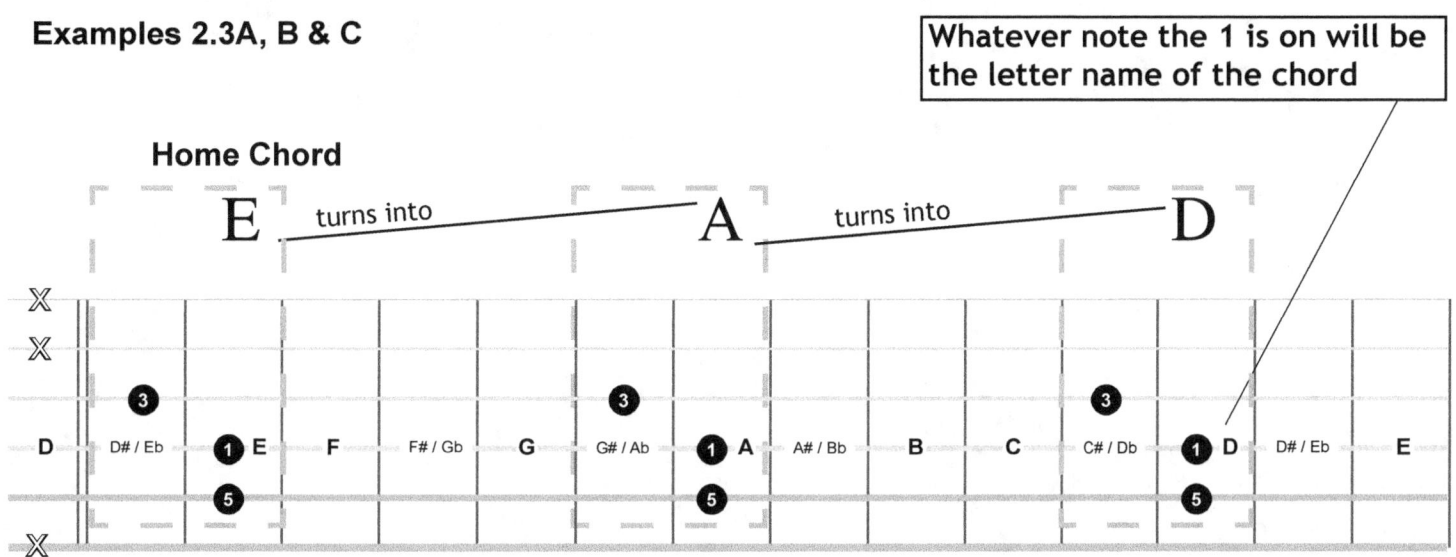

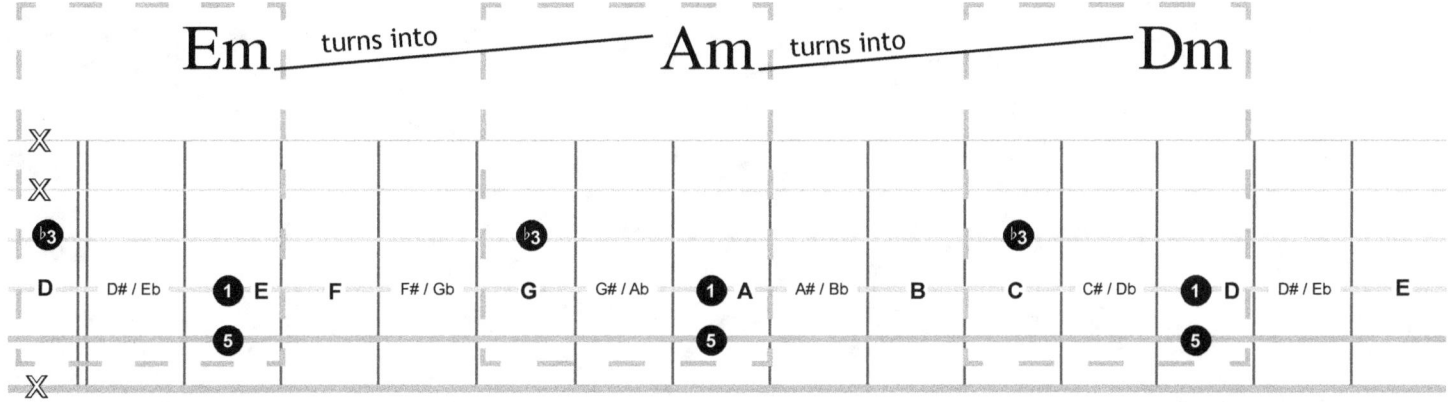

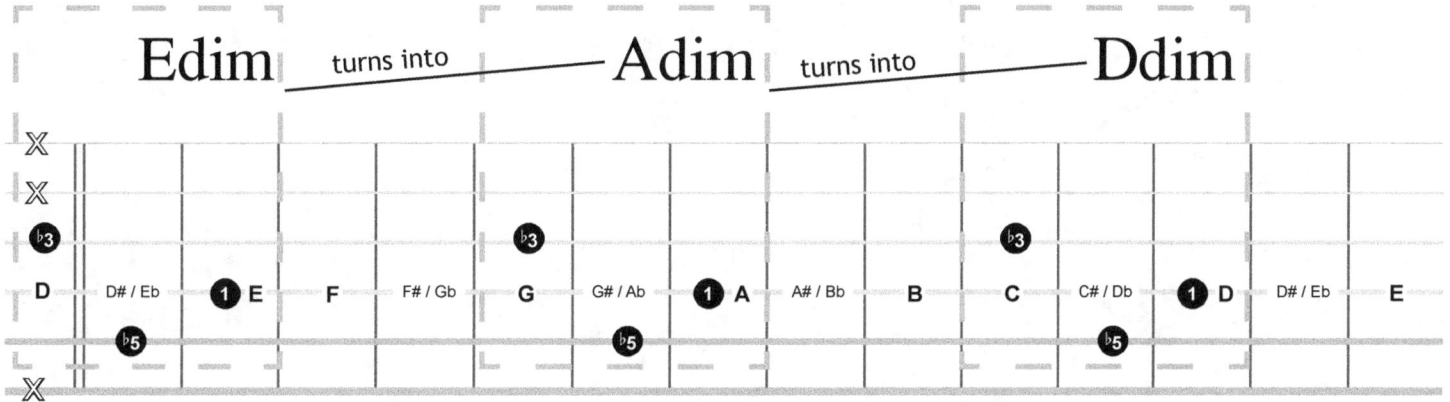

SECTION 3
Four-Note Chords

Home Chords

Major 7th Chords

Example 3.1

Notice that we still have a 1 in these chords, on an OPEN string

D

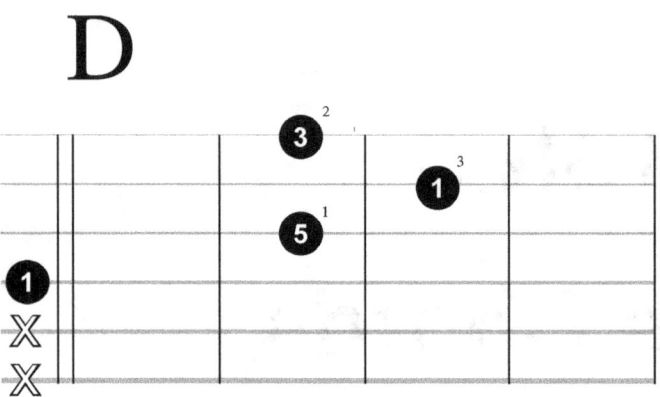

A

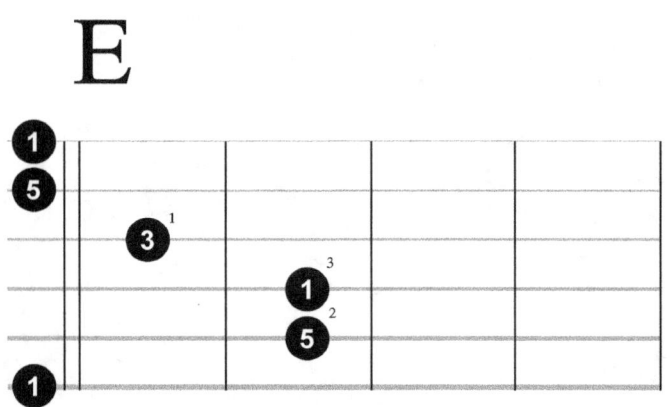

E

Dmaj⁷

Replace the 1st with the 7th

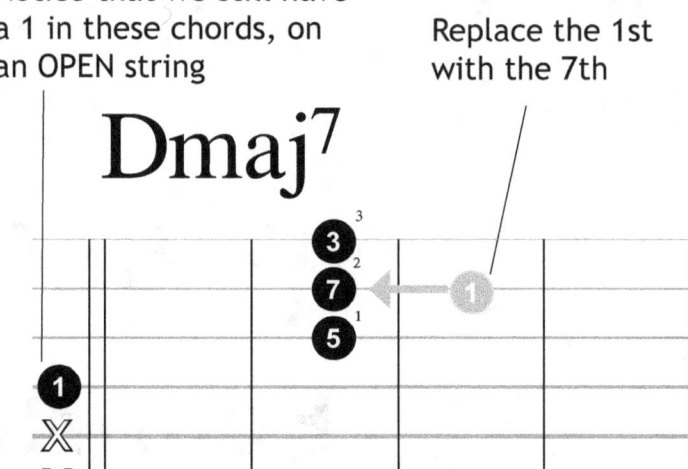

Amaj⁷

Replace the 1st with the 7th

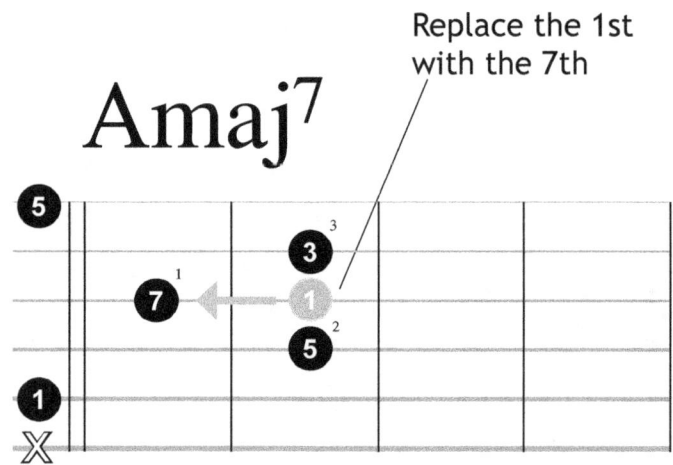

Emaj⁷

Replace the 1st with the 7th

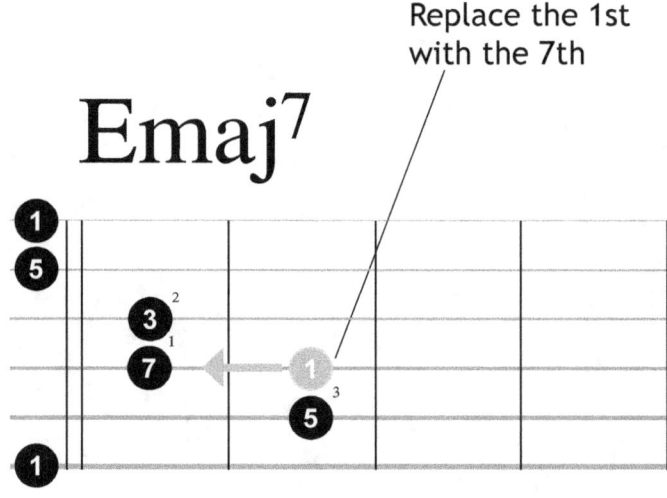

Major 7th Chords
1 - 3 - 5 - 7

When you feel that you've mastered the three-note chords we've covered, it's time to start on the four-note chords. Notice that the ($\frac{3}{1}$) pattern of our home chords has changed to become ($\frac{3}{7}$) in Example 3.1 by **replacing the 1 with the 7**. We still have a 1 in the chord, on an open string, making the formula for the Major 7th chords: 1,3,5,7. You may have also noted that the 7th is located one fret to the left of the 1, so it's just like "flatting the 1", although it's called a 7th, *not* a flat 1.

Practice going from the Major (Home) chords to the Major 7th a few times to get used to the fingering changes, then try the strumming exercises below:

Major 7th Chord Strumming

Amaj^7				Dmaj^7				Amaj^7				Dmaj^7			
‖: 1	2	3	4	1	2	3	4	1	2	3	4	1	2	3	4
strum				*strum*				*strum*							

Emaj^7				Amaj^7				Emaj^7				Amaj^7			
1	2	3	4	1	2	3	4	1	2	3	4	1	2	3	4 :‖

Now is a good time to review all of the formulas that we have learned so far on the list below. Try not to look back to the previous pages for help unless absolutely necessary.

1	3	5		Major
1	3	5	7	Major 7th
1	♭3	5		Minor
1	♭3	♭5		Diminished
1	3	♯5		Augmented

It is very important to know how to build the chords by using the scale degrees. That way, as long as you know the three Home chords, and remember that flat (♭) = 1 fret left and sharp (♯) = 1 fret right, you can figure out the other chords from the formulas.

In time, these formulas will be as easy to remember as a few telephone numbers.

Home Chords

Dominant 7th Chords

Example 3.2

D

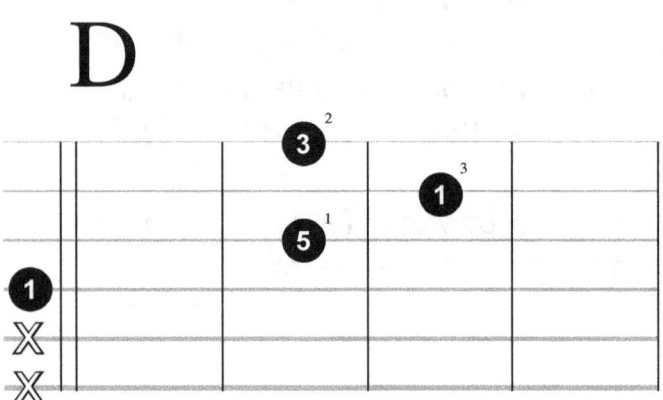

D⁷

Flat the 7th

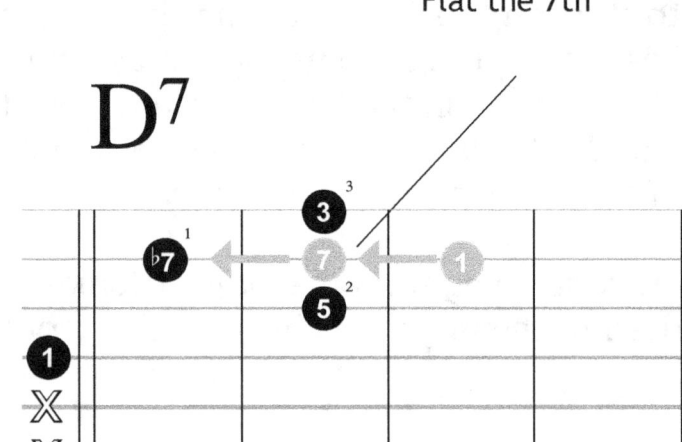

A

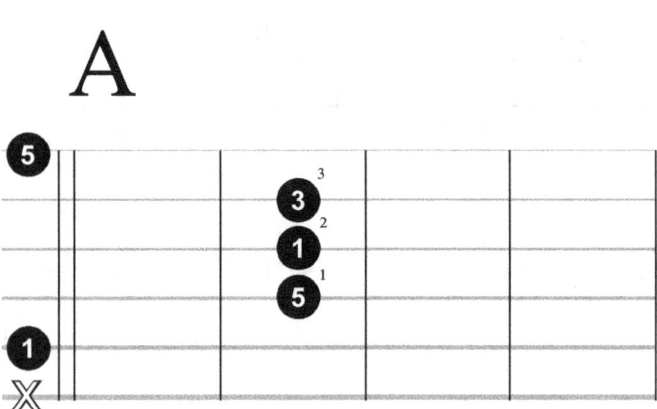

A⁷

Flat the 7th

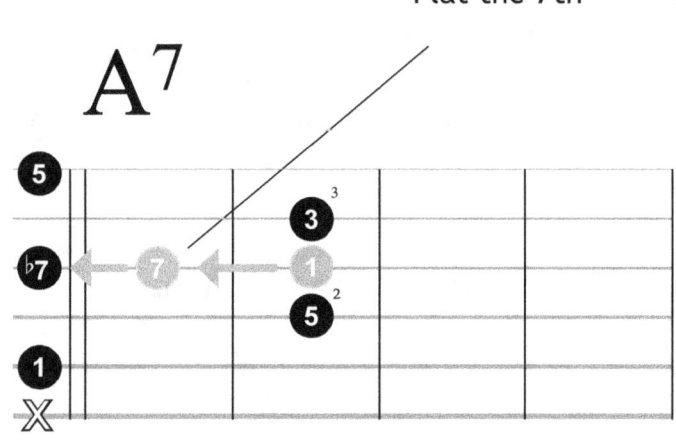

E

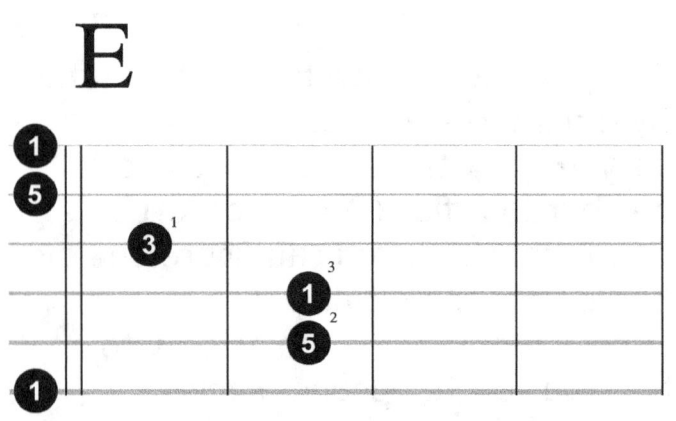

E⁷

Flat the 7th

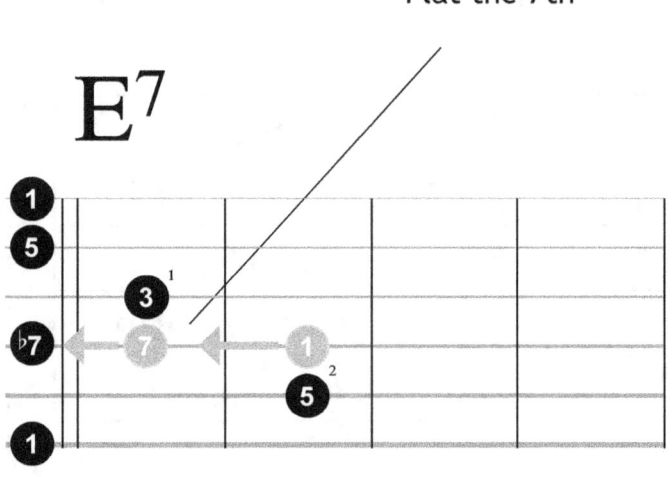

Dominant 7th Chords
1 - 3 - 5 - ♭7

Our next chords, shown in Example 3.2, are the Dominant 7th chords. We start at the Home chords as usual, replace the 1st with a 7th, then flat the 7th, making the formula: 1, 3, 5, ♭7.

Practice going from D to D7 a few times, then do the same with the other chords. When you are comfortable with the fingering changes, try the 12-bar blues progression shown below.

12 Bar Dominant 7th Blues

A^7 | D^7 | A^7 |
| :1 2 3 4 | 1 2 3 4 | 1 2 3 4 | 1 2 3 4 |
| *strum* | *strum* | *strum* | |

D^7 | | A^7 | |
| 1 2 3 4 | 1 2 3 4 | 1 2 3 4 | 1 2 3 4 |

E^7 | D^7 | A^7 | E^7 |
| 1 2 3 4 | 1 2 3 4 | 1 2 3 4 | 1 2 3 4: |

Home Chords

Minor 7th Chords

Example 3.3

D

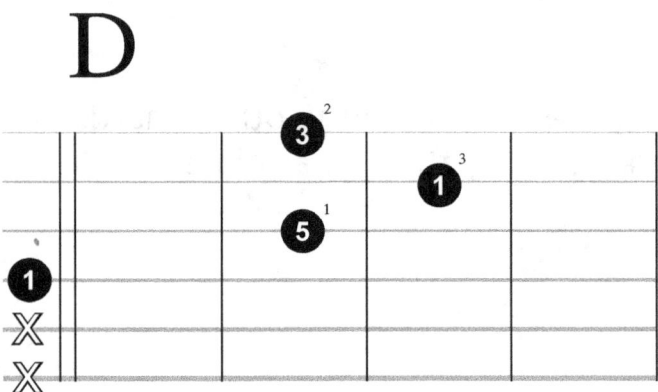

Dm⁷

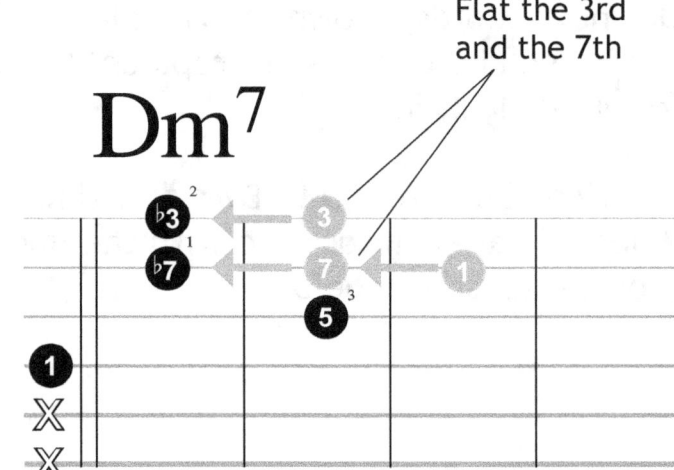

Flat the 3rd and the 7th

A

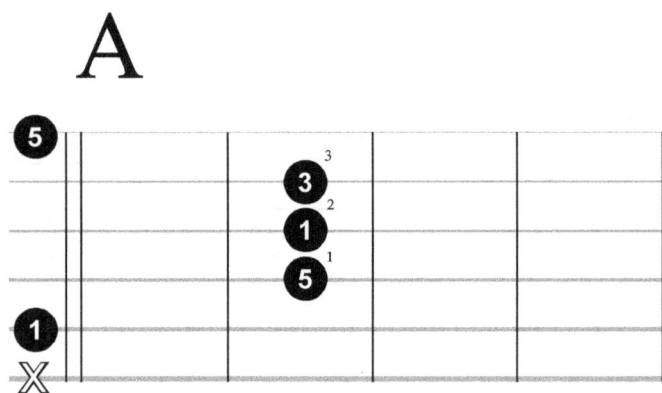

Am⁷

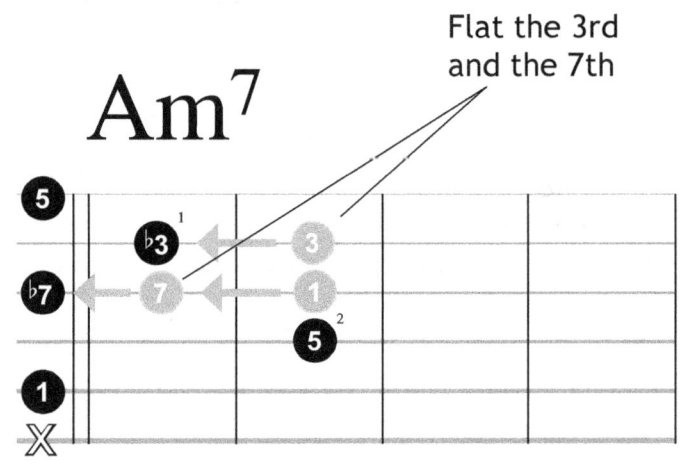

Flat the 3rd and the 7th

E

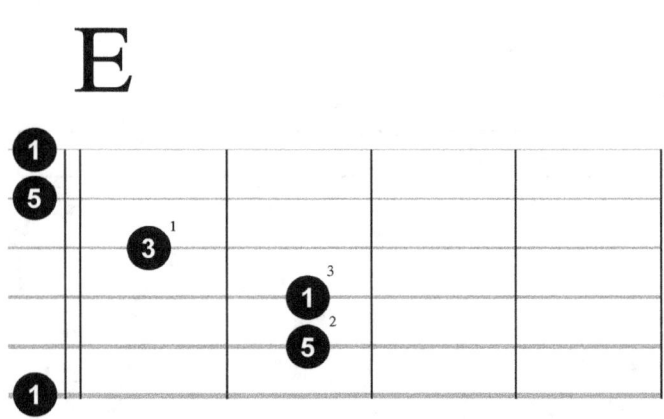

Em⁷

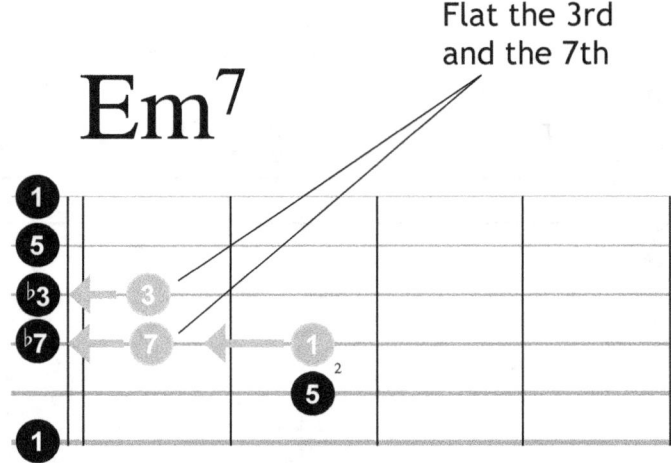

Flat the 3rd and the 7th

Minor 7th Chords
1 - ♭3 - 5 - ♭7

Now try our 12 Bar Blues with the Minor 7th chords. To make the Minor 7th chords, we start at the Home chords, replace the 1st with a 7th, then flat the 3rd and the 7th as shown in Example 3.3, making the formula: 1, ♭3, 5, ♭7.

You'll probably like the Em7 chord - since both the flat 3 and flat 7 are on open strings, it's especially easy to make!

12 Bar Minor 7th Blues

Am⁷				Dm⁷				Am⁷							
‖: 1	2	3	4	1	2	3	4	1	2	3	4	1	2	3	4
strum				*strum*				*strum*							

Dm⁷								Am⁷							
1	2	3	4	1	2	3	4	1	2	3	4	1	2	3	4

Em⁷				Dm⁷				Am⁷				Em⁷			
1	2	3	4	1	2	3	4	1	2	3	4	1	2	3	4 :‖

Home Chords

D

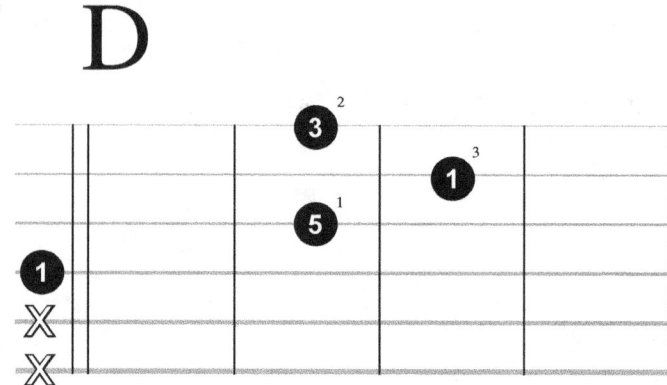

A

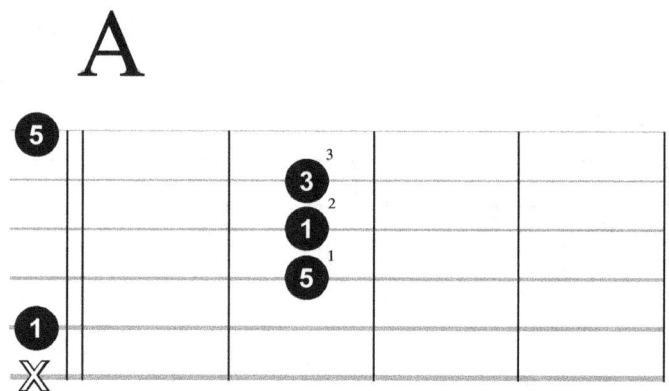

E

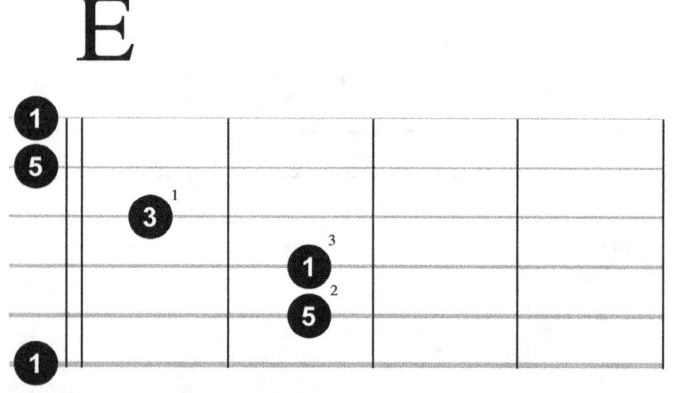

Minor 7th (♭5) Chords

Example 3.4

Dm⁷⁽♭⁵⁾

Flat the 3rd, 5th and 7th

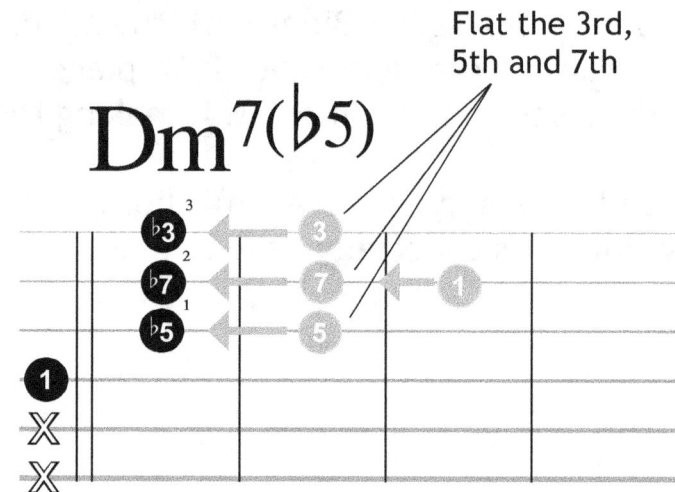

Am⁷⁽♭⁵⁾

Flat the 3rd, 5th and 7th

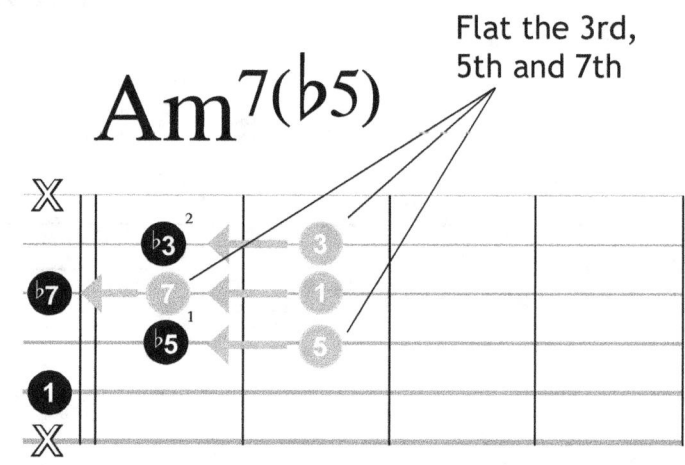

Em⁷⁽♭⁵⁾

Flat the 3rd, 5th and 7th

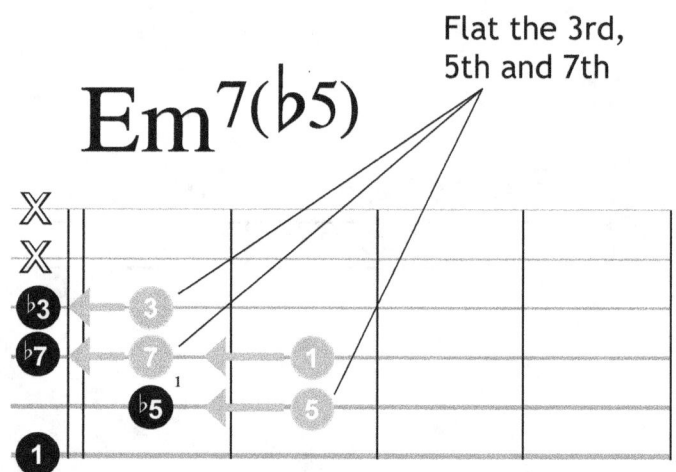

Minor 7th ($\flat$5) Chords
1 - $\flat$3 - $\flat$5 - $\flat$7

The last chords in this section will be the Minor 7th ($\flat$5) ("Minor 7 Flat 5") chords. These are produced by starting at the home chords, replacing the 1st with a 7th, then flat the 3rd, 5th and 7th as shown in Example 3.4, giving us the formula of 1, $\flat$3, $\flat$5, $\flat$7. Notice on the $Am^{7(\flat5)}$ and $Em^{7(\flat5)}$ that you no longer strum some of the open strings you've been used to strumming.

Example 3.5

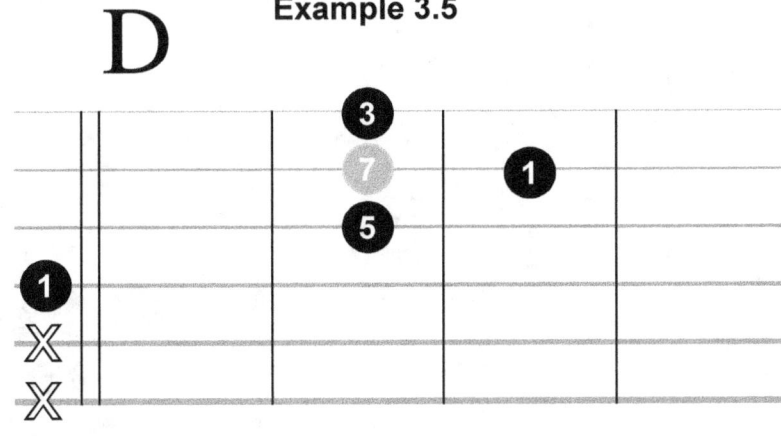

Review
8 Formulas = 24 Chords

Now let's see if you can figure out all of the different types of D, A and E chords, using only the charts in Example 3.5 and the list of chord formulas below.

Remember that
flat ($\flat$) = 1 fret left
sharp ($\sharp$) = 1 fret right

1		3		5			Major
1	$\flat$3		5				Minor
1	$\flat$3		$\flat$5				Diminished
1		3	$\sharp$5				Augmented
1		3		5	7		Major 7th
1		3		5	$\flat$7		Dominant 7th
1	$\flat$3		5		$\flat$7		Minor 7th
1	$\flat$3		$\flat$5		$\flat$7		Minor 7th $^{(\flat5)}$

SECTION 4

Sliding 4-Note Chords
Without the Root

Example 4 shows the names of the notes on the second, third and fourth strings of the guitar. You learned these notes in Section 2 of the book. If you've forgotten them, take some time to refresh your memory before proceeding.

Example 4

		1		3		5		7		9			12		
2nd String	B	C	C#/Db	D	D#/Eb	E	F	F#/Gb	G	G#/Ab	A	A#/Bb	B	C	C#/Db
3rd String	G	G#/Ab	A	A#/Bb	B	C	C#/Db	D	D#/Eb	E	F	F#/Gb	G	G#/Ab	A
4th String	D	D#/Eb	E	F	F#/Gb	G	G#/Ab	A	A#/Bb	B	C	C#/Db	D	D#/Eb	E

In this section, we're going to learn how to slide our 4-note chord formulas up and down the neck of the guitar to create new chords.

With our 4-note chords, we replaced the 1 (root) with the 7 and played the 1 on an open string. When we slide these chords, you still need to be aware of where the 1 is located, since this will determine the letter name of the new chord.

Since we can't slide open string notes, we leave those out (Example 4.1) and just slide three notes. Even though our new chords won't have the 1, they'll still function as a substitute for the named chord.

Later on when we work on bar chords, we'll be adding the root back into the chord.

Study Examples 4.2A through 4.4C

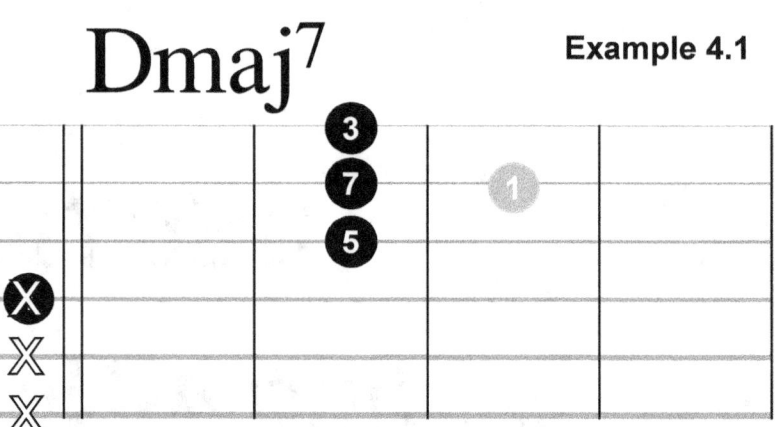

Dmaj⁷   **Example 4.1**

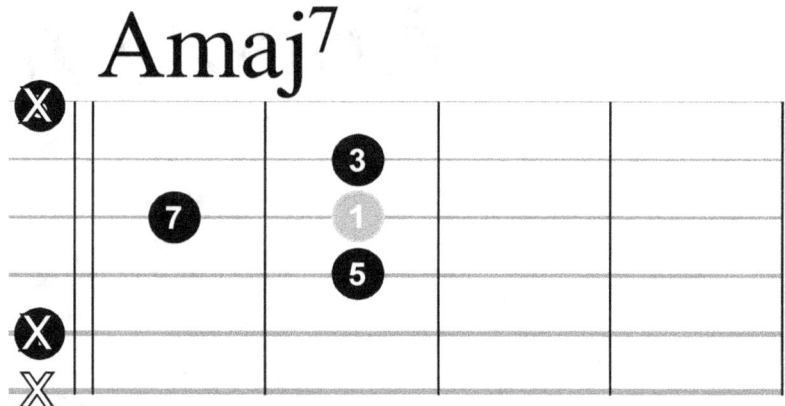

Amaj⁷

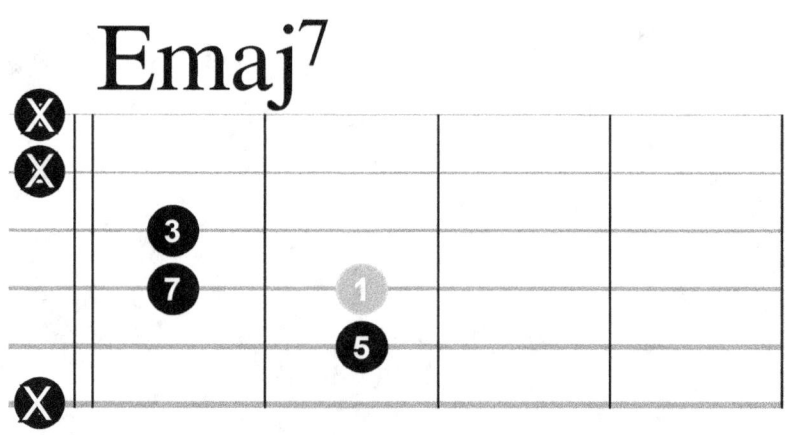

Emaj⁷

Page 34

Examples 4.2A, B & C show how to slide 3 notes of the 4-note D chord formulas up and down the neck of the guitar. Even though we're playing a 7 instead of a 1, the letter name of the new chord is determined by where the 1 *would be* in the new chord. Remember that we won't be playing the notes on the X-ed out open strings in our new chords.

Examples 4.2A, B & C

Whatever note the 1 *would be* on will be the letter name of the chord

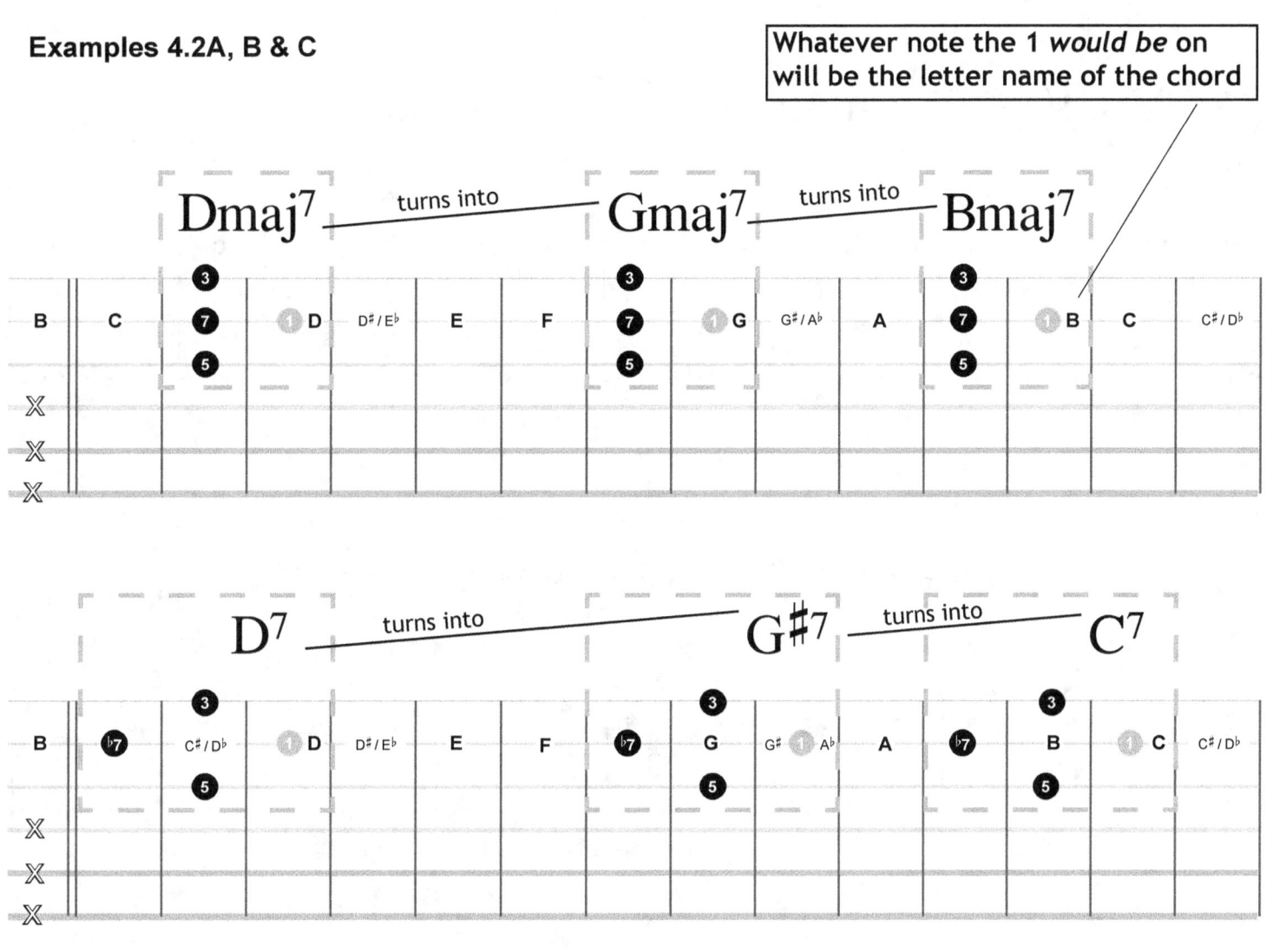

Now we'll slide 3 notes of the 4-note A chords to create new chords. Notice that I still have all the open strings X-ed out - you shouldn't strum those.

Examples 4.3A, B & C

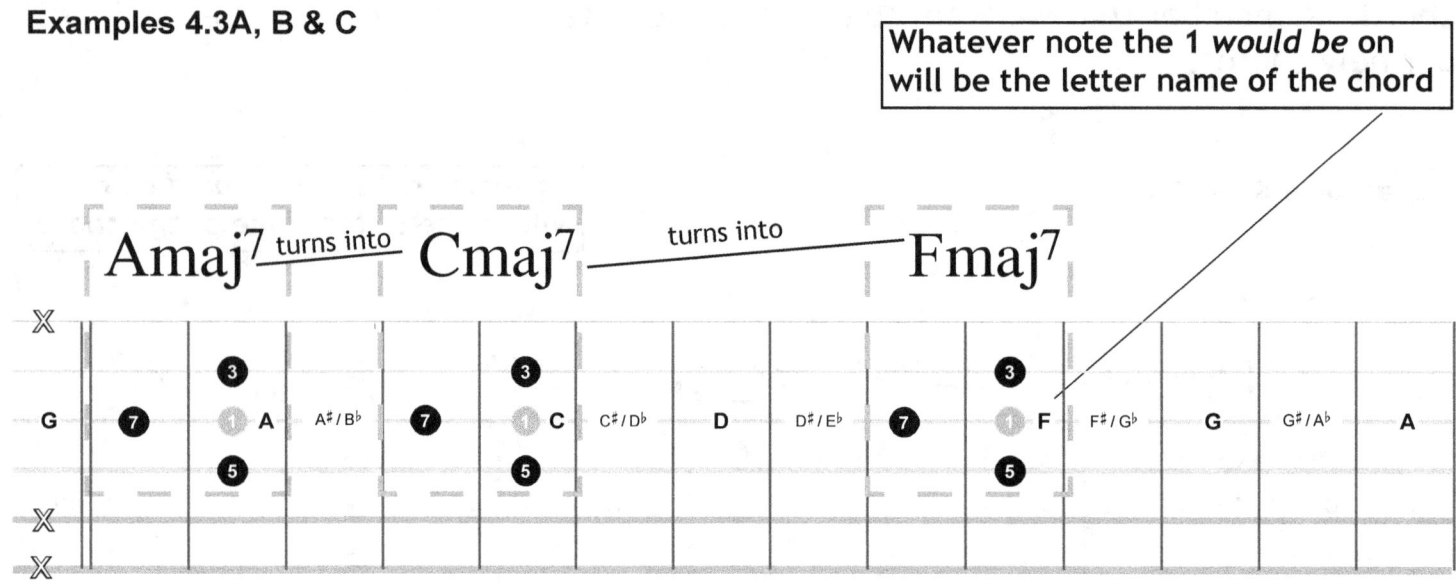

Whatever note the 1 *would be* on will be the letter name of the chord

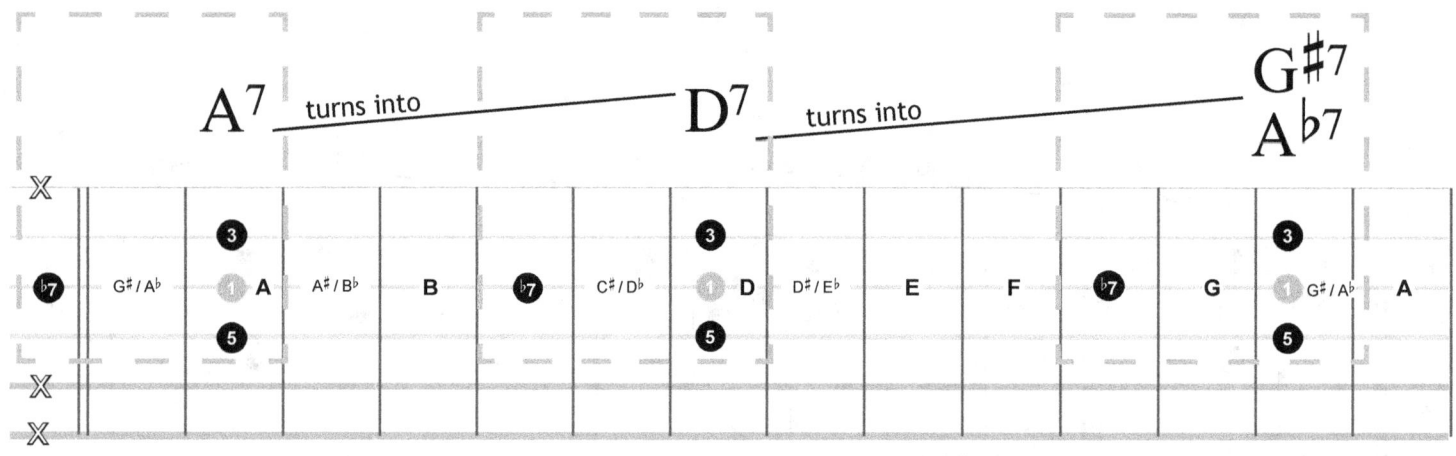

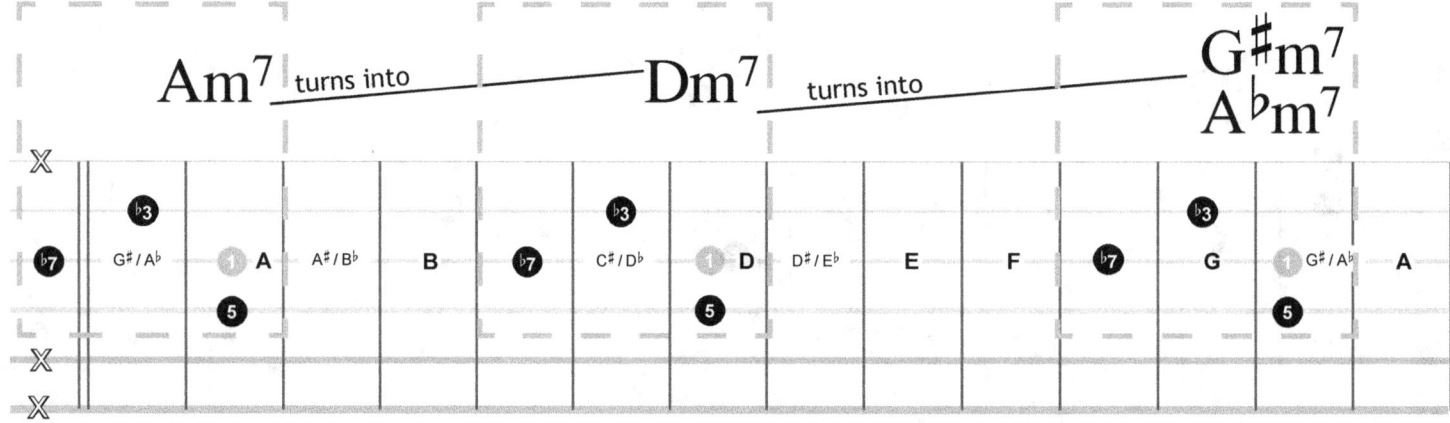

Finally, let's do the same thing with our four-note E chords. The open strings that you shouldn't strum are X-ed out and now we use the notes on the **fourth** string (where the root (1) of the E Chord is located) to find the letter name of the new chords.

Examples 4.3A, B & C

Whatever note the 1 *would be* on will be the letter name of the chord

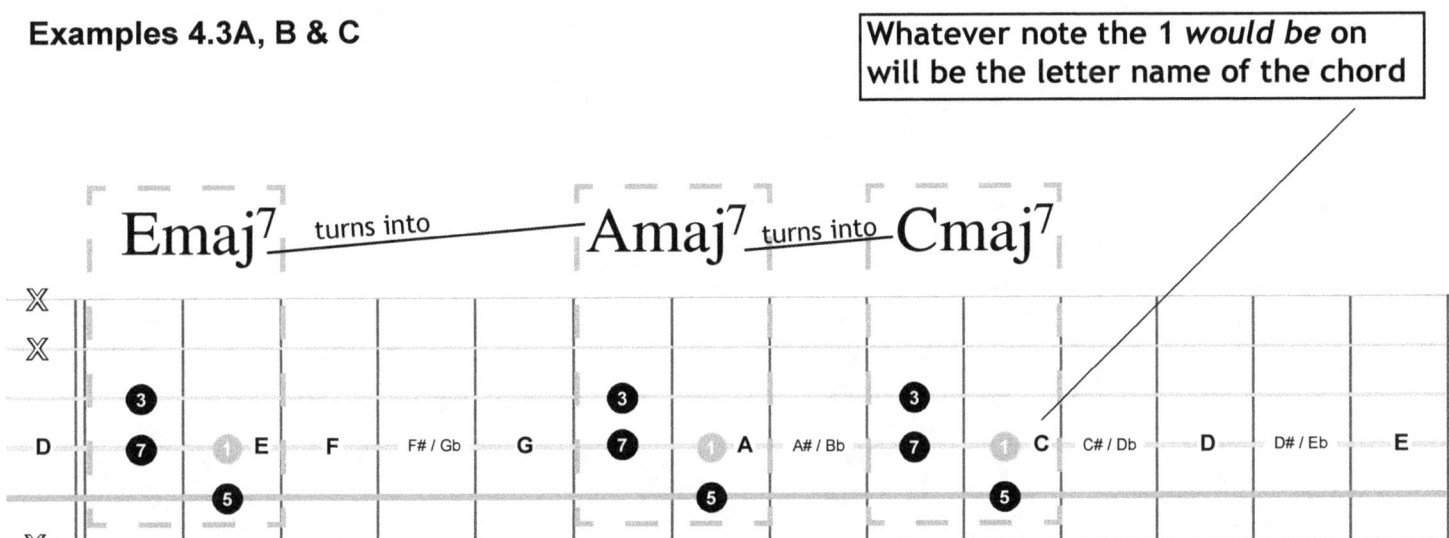

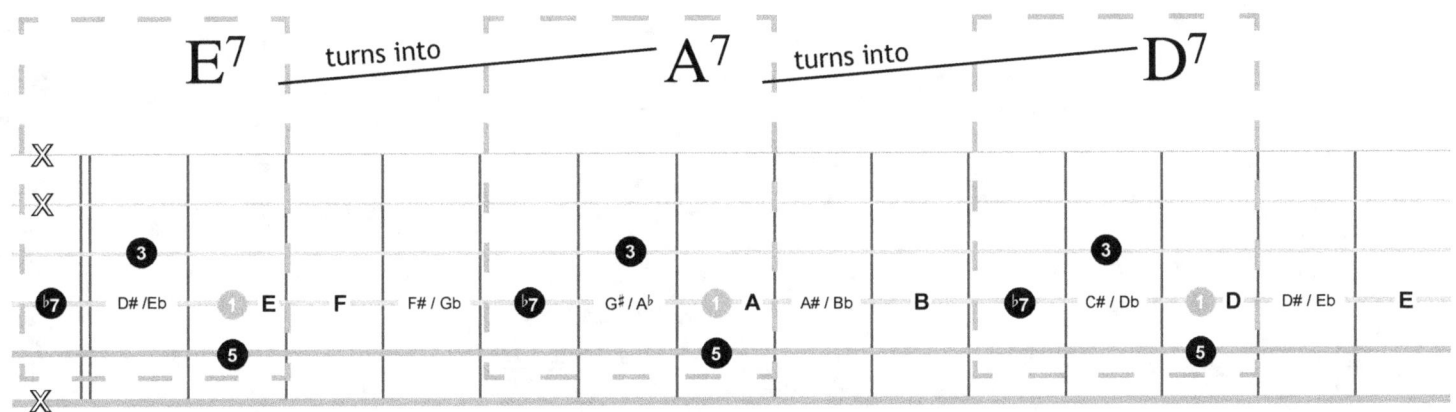

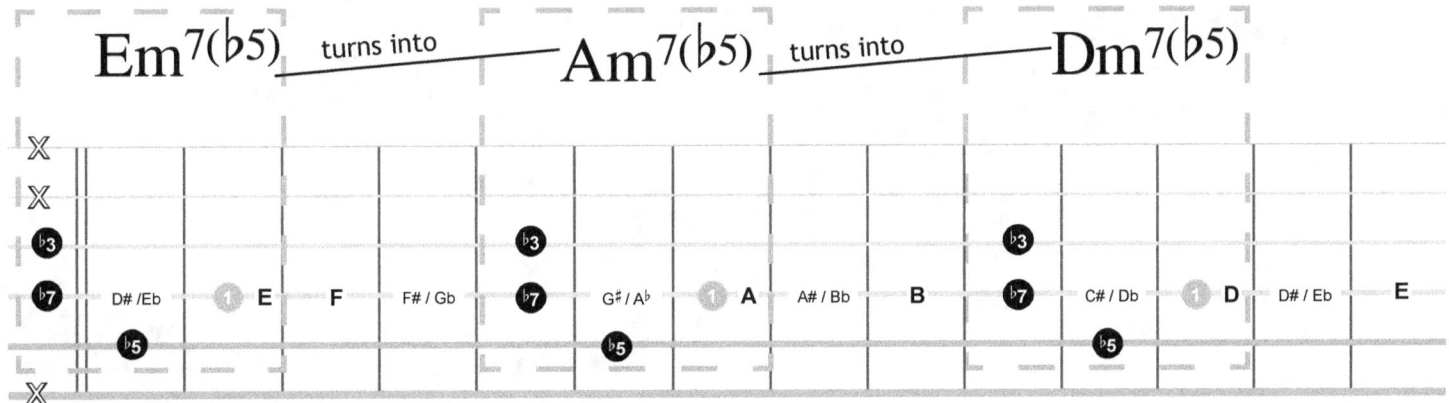

SECTION 5
Barre Chords

Introduction to Barre Chords

Remember that when sliding our 3-note chords, we did not play any open strings, since we can't slide open string notes? And when we slid the 4-note chords, we had to leave out the 1 (root), since it was on an open string, and we can't slide open string notes.

Barre chords (also called "bar" chords) give us a way to slide our open string notes. When making barre chords, you use your index finger to press down on multiple strings at once, like a bar pressing down on the strings. In a sense, your index finger becomes the nut of the guitar.

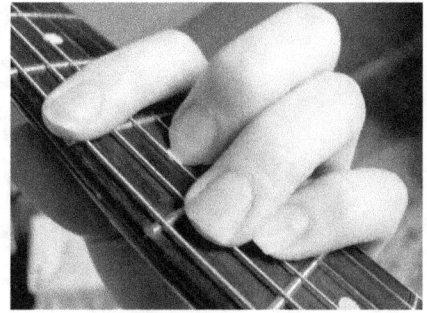

When making a barre chord, make sure your thumb is directly behind your index finger on the back of the guitar neck. This will help you apply maximum pressure. The most challenging part of making barre chords is getting your finger to press down evenly across all the string, hard enough so that all the strings ring out and aren't muted. Practice barring all 6 strings with your index finger until you develop the strength and flexibility to make all the strings ring out. It can take a while to master this skill, so be patient and practice consistently.

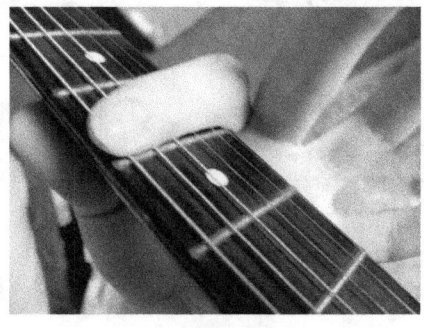

First we will start by turning the home E chord in the example below into a barre chord, in this case A and then D. We will have to make our E chord first but the normal fingerings that we used earlier for this chord will have to change so we can free up the index finger for barring. Once you have all of your fingers in the right places, try sliding the whole chord to the right 5 frets and then bar by laying your first finger flat across all six strings on the fifth fret (see example below). This will produce an A barre chord. Then if you slide that chord to the right five more frets it will turn into a D chord. This same concept will apply to all the different types of D, A and E chords, as shown in the following examples.

Bar with the first finger by laying it flat across all six strings on the fifth fret.

Remember that whatever note the 1 is on will be the letter name of the chord. You'll often have more than one root (1) in a chord, but they'll all fall on the same note.

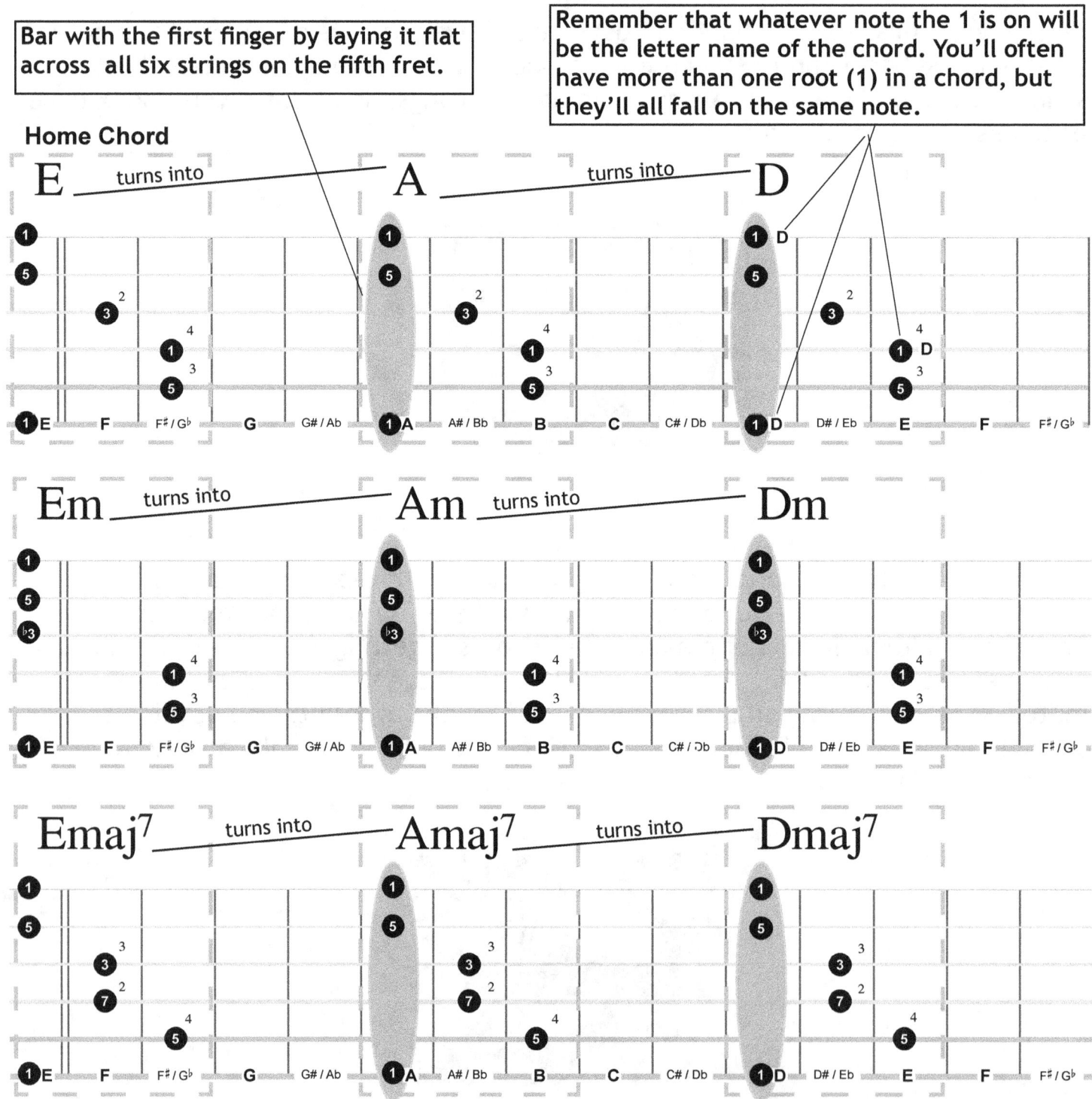

Page 42

Now lets try making the A chord using the alternate fingering (in the example below) and then sliding the whole A chord five frets to the right to turn into a D barre chord. This time there is no need to bar the sixth string since we won't be strumming it.

Bar by laying the first finger flat across the bottom 5 strings on the fifth fret. Remember that the 1 determines the letter name of the chord.

Examples 5.2A, B & C

Home Chord

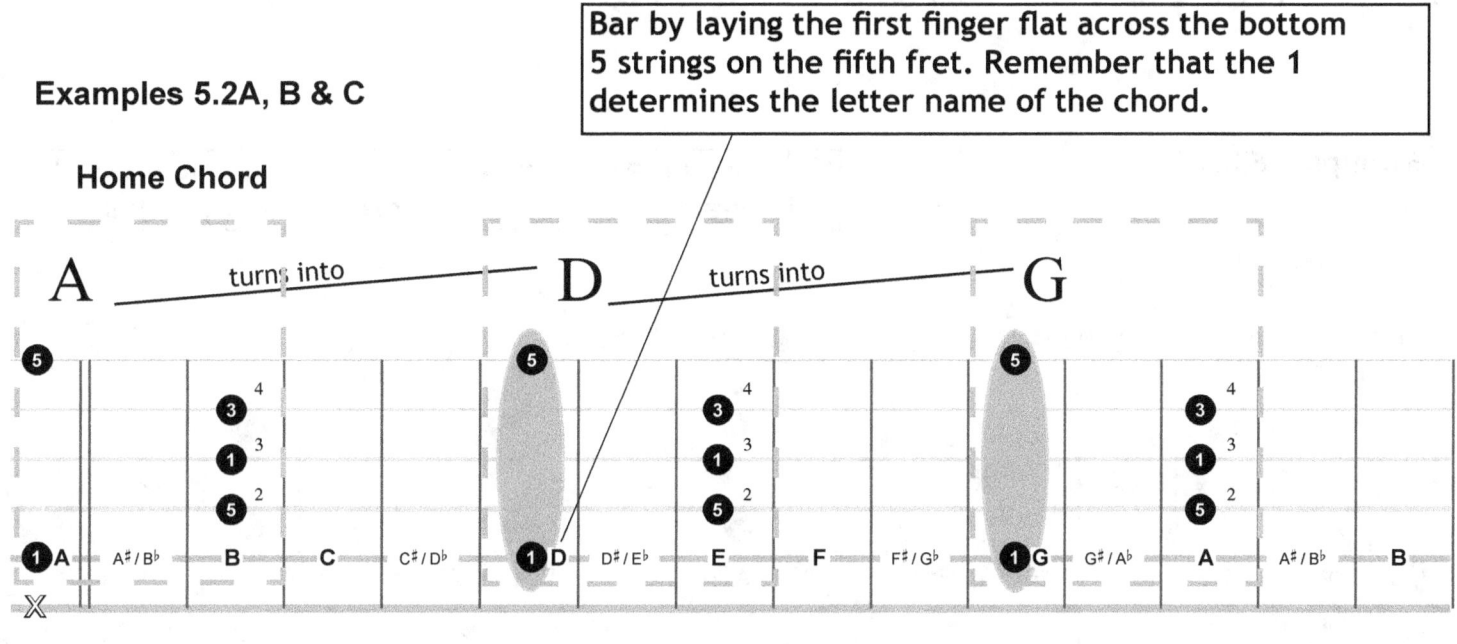

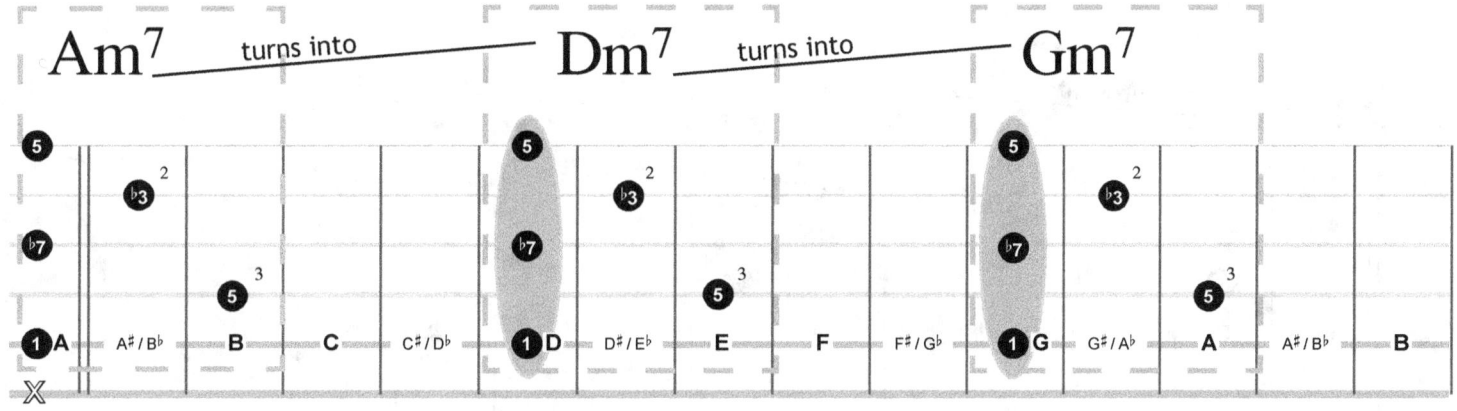

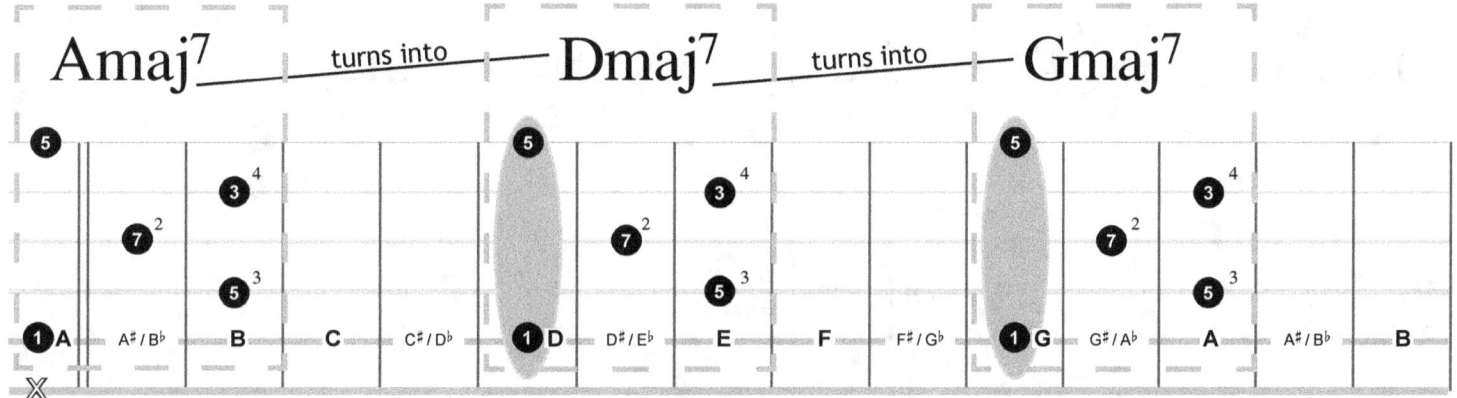

With the D chord, there's only one open string note that is played. So when we slide the full chord, there's no need to bar multiple stings. However, you still need to use alternate fingerings (see the example below) to free up your index finger so you can use it to fret the note that was on the open string.

Examples 5.3A, B & C

Use your index finger for this note, but since there's only one note in this fret, there's no need to bar.

Home Chord

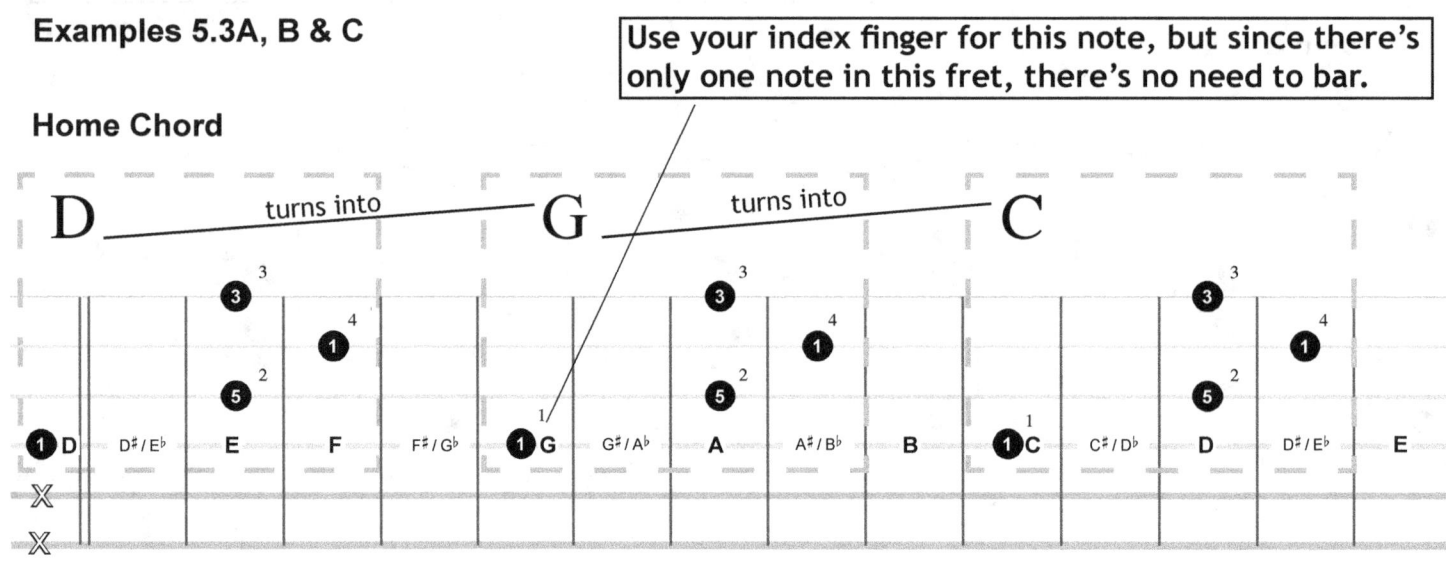

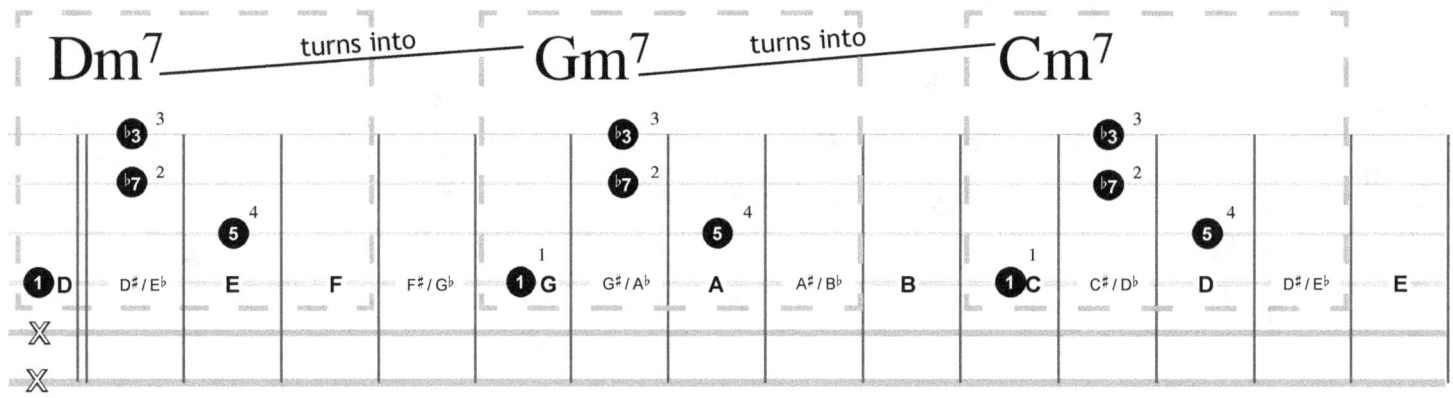

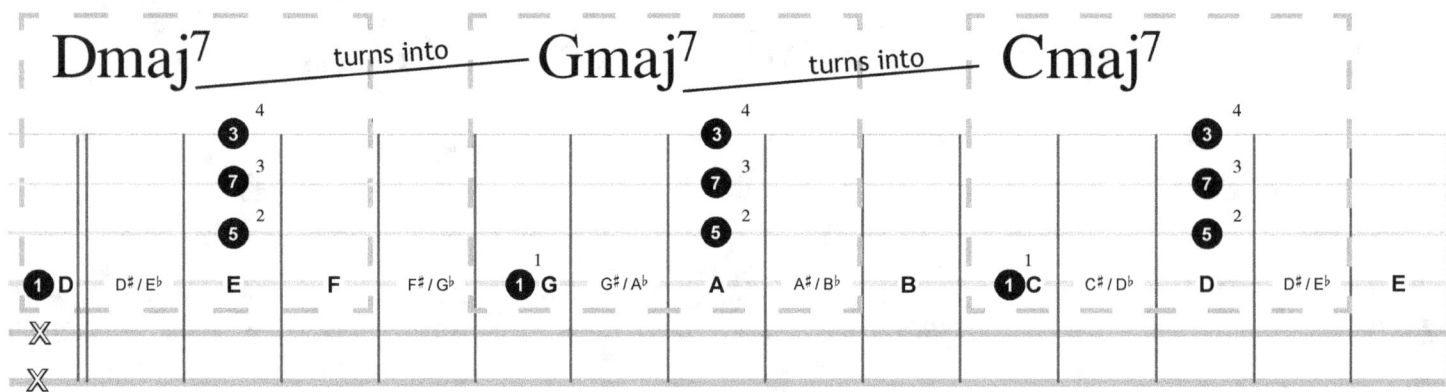

Chords that are Difficult To Convert Into Barre Chords

Example 5.4

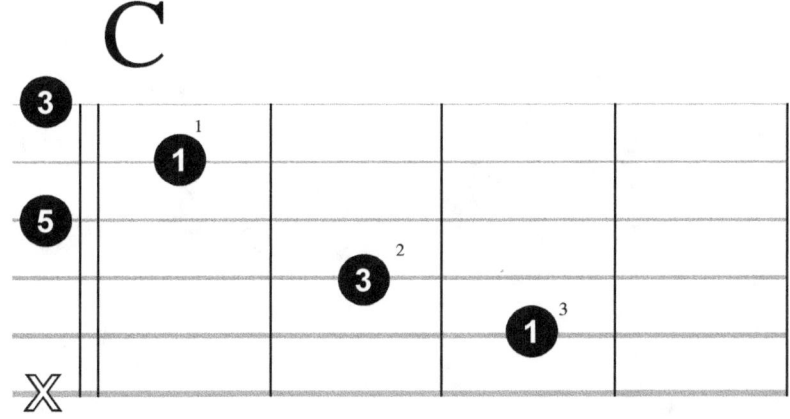

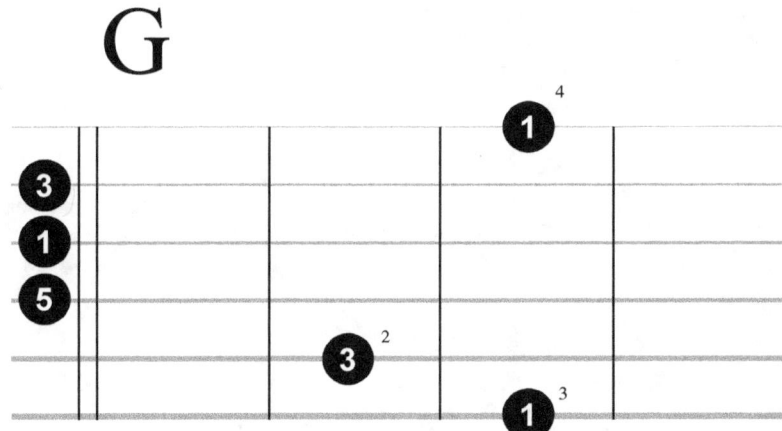

So far, we've dealt with only the D, A & E chords. We've seen that these chords all move around the guitar in similar ways and that from them, we can create all of the other chords that we need.

However, we're going to give a couple of other chords, the C and G chords, special mention here, since they are chords that many beginning guitarists have already learned. Example 5.4 shows the traditional fingerings for the C and G chords.

Although you can create a C or G chord by sliding and barring the D, A or E chords, the barred versions do not ring out quite as well and are much harder to play. So if I have a choice, I play the C and G chords using the fingering shown in Example 5.4 to give my barring finger a little break.

The problem with these chords is that they are very difficult to slide up and down the neck in their present form, unless you break the chords up into smaller fragments that you wont have to barre.

SECTION 6
Chord Inversions

Major Chords with Scale Degrees

Some D Major Chord Inversions

D Example 6.1

D Examples 6.2A, B, C, D, E

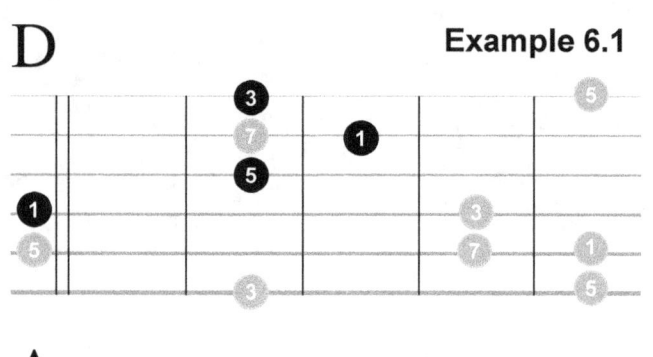

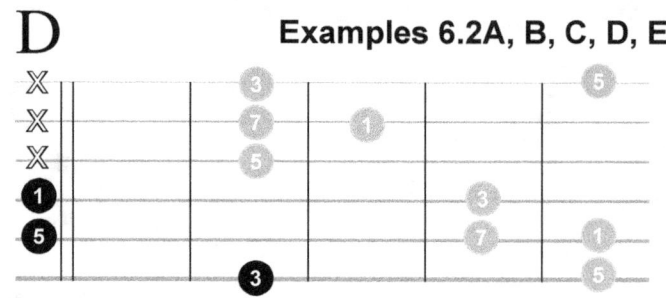

A

D

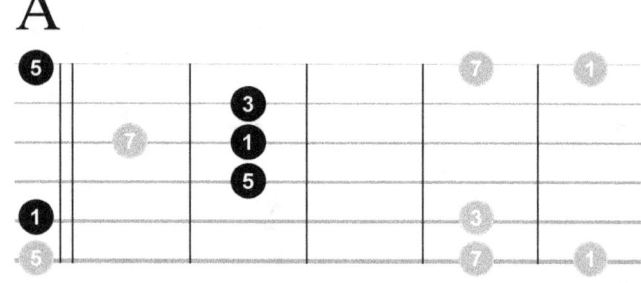

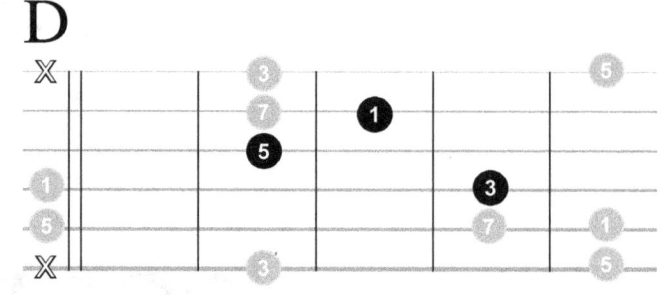

E

D

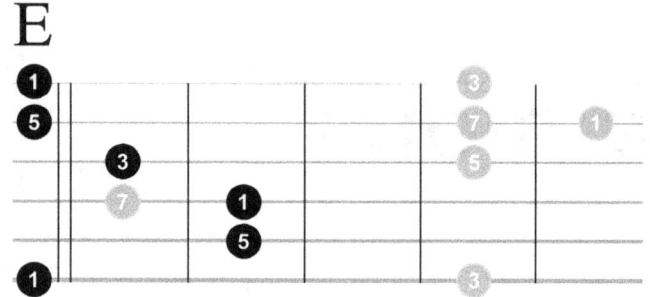

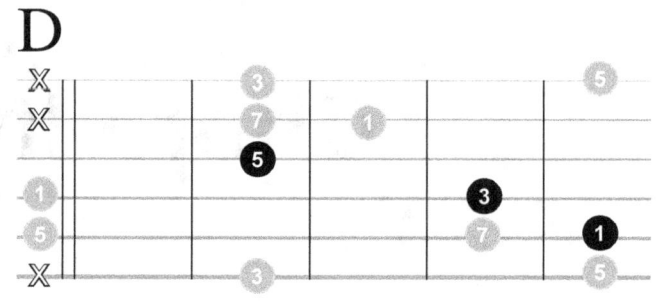

C

D

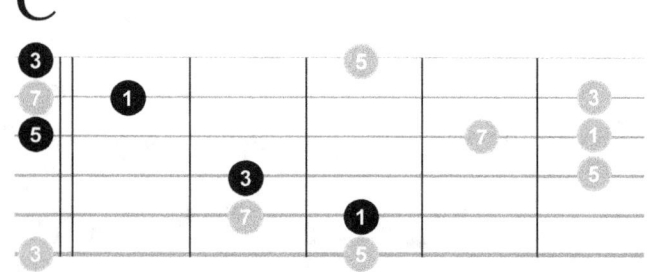

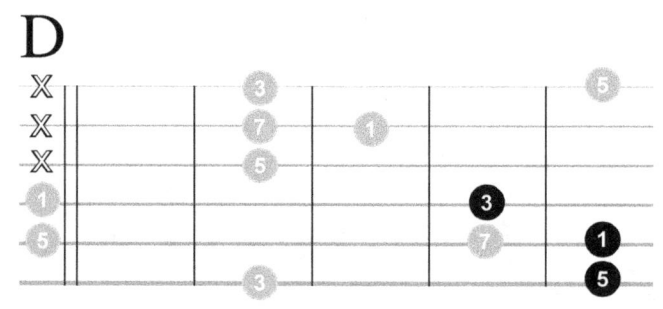

G

D

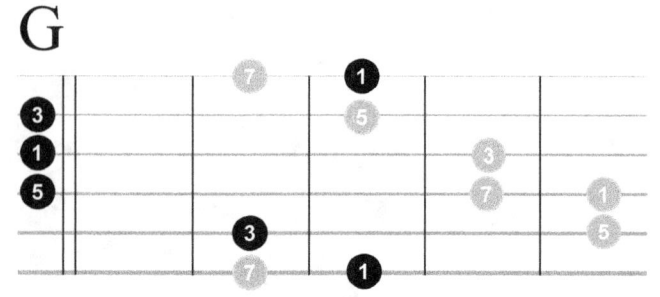

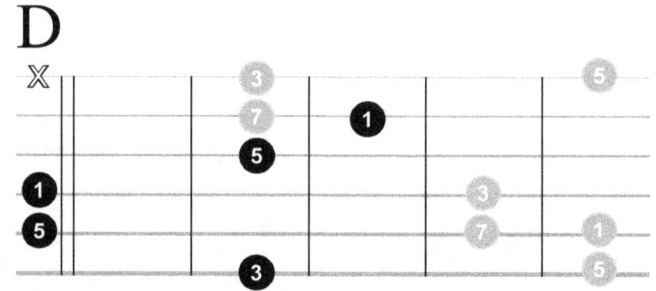

Chord Inversions

Example 6.1 shows all of the 1, 3, 5 and 7 scale degrees for each chord on the first 5 frets of the guitar. We can use these to make different *inversions* of all of the chords we have learned.

Starting with the D Major chord try to find different ways to combine the 1, 3 and 5 scale degrees in different order to make what are called chord inversions. Any combination of 1-3-5 (3-5-1; 5-1-3, etc.), will count as a D Major chord as long as you have the three scale degrees present and each is on a separate string so that you can strum them together.

As a beginner, you should look for combinations on sequential strings, so that you don't have to be concerned with the notes on any strings you aren't fretting (open strings) - you won't strum those strings, as in Example 6.2A,B,C & D.

After you feel comfortable with the D Major chord, try the same exercise with the other Major chords before you attempt the list below. As you progress, you can explore inversions using notes on non-sequential strings and with more than 3 notes. If an open string has a scale degree that's already part of your chord, you can strum it, as in Example 6.2E. If it has a scale degree that you don't want in your chord, you can try to mute it, or play your chord as an *arpeggio*. An arpeggio is when you pick each note of the chord individually instead of strumming the chord.

This should keep you busy for quite awhile and will help you to get familiar with where the scale degrees are located on the neck of your guitar.

Remember that
flat (♭) = 1 fret left
sharp (♯) = 1 fret right

1	3	5		Major
1	♭3	5		Minor
1	♭3	♭5		Diminished
1	3	♯5		Augmented
1	3	5	7	Major 7th
1	3	5	♭7	Dominant 7th
1	♭3	5	♭7	Minor 7th
1	♭3	♭5	♭7	Minor 7th (♭5)

SECTION 7

Using the Major Scale
to Create More Chords

Example 7.1

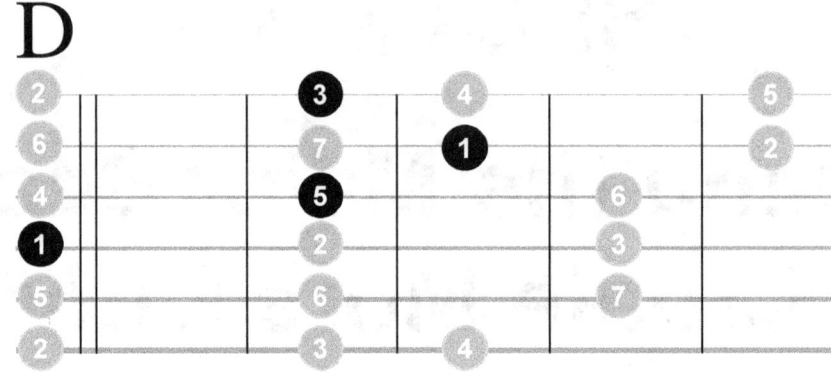

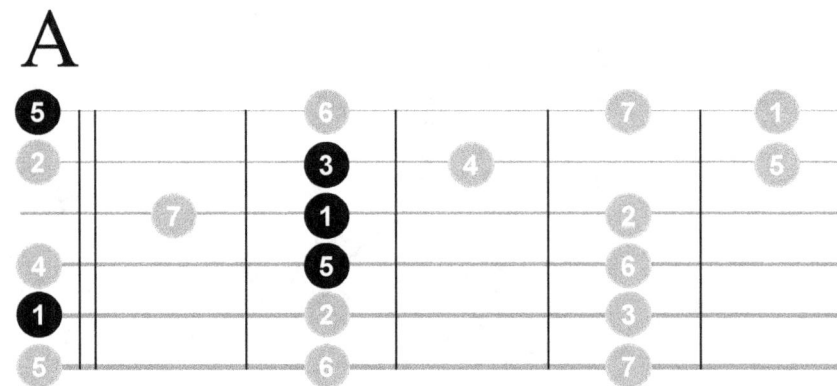

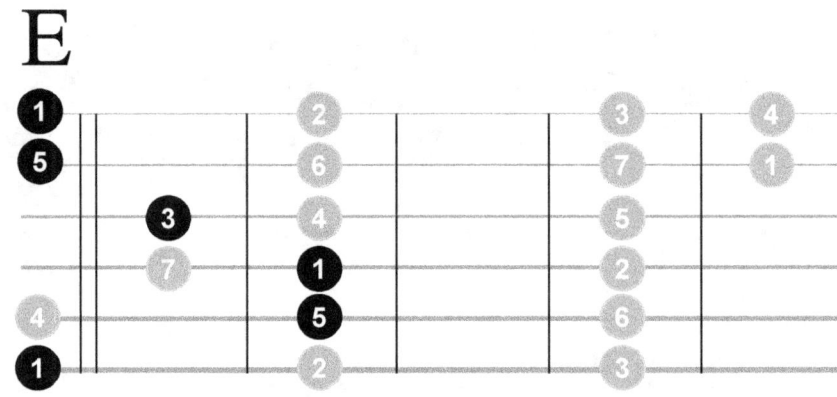

Making Chords from the Major Scale

In the last section we mentioned arpeggios. An arpeggio is when you pick each note of the chord individually instead of strumming the chord. Now that you are acquainted with this concept, the next step is to add in the missing scale degrees: **2, 4, & 6** which creates the seven digit formula of **1-2-3-4-5-6-7** (the Major Scale). This scale will open the door to a lot of other chords that we haven't gone over yet.

Below are the chord formulas we have already learned, and some new chord formulas to experiment with.

flat ($\flat$) = 1 fret left
double flat ($\flat\flat$) = 2 frets left
sharp ($\sharp$) = 1 fret right

Chord Formula	Name	How it's Written
1 3 5	Major	D
1 $\flat$3 5	Minor	Dm
1 $\flat$3 $\flat$5	Diminished	Ddim
1 3 $\sharp$5	Augmented	Daug
1 3 5 7	Major 7th	Dmaj^7
1 3 5 $\flat$7	Dominant 7th	D^7
1 $\flat$3 5 $\flat$7	Minor 7th	Dm^7
1 $\flat$3 $\flat$5 $\flat$7	Minor 7 $^{(\flat 5)}$	Dm$^{7\flat 5}$
1 3 5 6	Major 6	D^6
1 $\flat$3 5 6	Minor 6	Dm^6
1 $\flat$3 $\flat$5 $\flat\flat$7 (or 6)	Diminished 7	Ddim^7
1 3 $\sharp$5 $\flat$7	Augmented 7	Daug^7
1 4 5	Suspended 4	Dsus^4
1 2 5	Suspended 2	Dsus^2

APPENDIX
Reference Charts

Reference Chart
The Three "Home Chords"

D

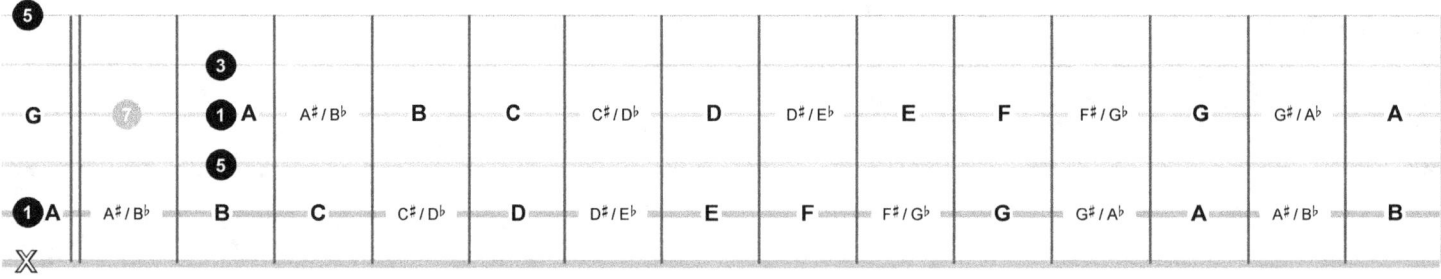

A

E

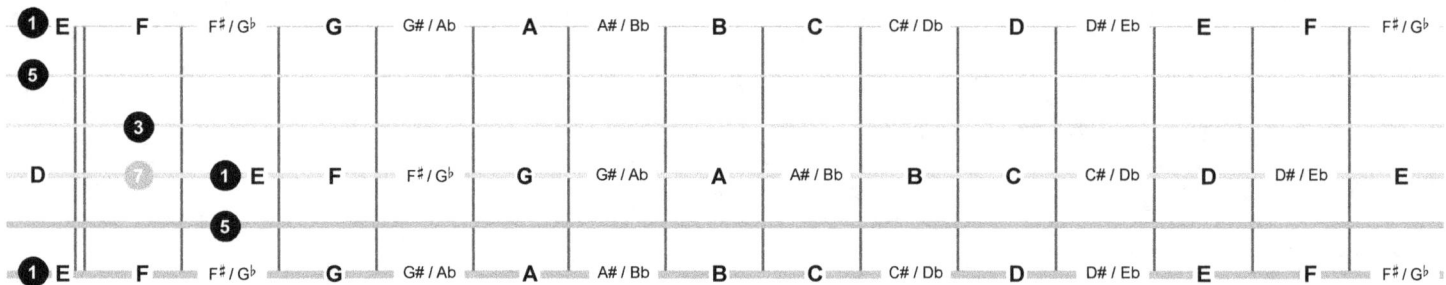

Reference Chart
Chord Formulas

Chord Formula	Name	How it's Written
1　3　5	Major	D
1　♭3　5	Minor	Dm
1　♭3　♭5	Diminished	Ddim
1　3　♯5	Augmented	Daug
1　3　5　7	Major 7th	$Dmaj^7$
1　3　5　♭7	Dominant 7th	D^7
1　♭3　5　♭7	Minor 7th	Dm^7
1　♭3　♭5　♭7	Minor 7 (♭5)	$Dm^{7♭5}$
1　3　5　6	Major 6	D^6
1　♭3　5　6	Minor 6	Dm^6
1　♭3　♭5　♭♭7 (or 6)	Diminished 7	$Ddim^7$
1　3　♯5　♭7	Augmented 7	$Daug^7$
1　4　5	Suspended 4	$Dsus^4$
1　2　5	Suspended 2	$Dsus^2$
1　5	Power Chord	D^5